1988

KIET

Creating and Painting in Watercolor

. . . a simple method for developing both creative and technical skills.
For the beginning and advanced painter.

Creating and Painting in Watercolor

by Carl Nickel

Doubleday & Company, Inc., Garden City, New York, 1972

Library of Congress Catalog Card Number 79–150909
Copyright © 1972 by Carl Nickel
All Rights Reserved
Printed in the United States of America
9   8   7   6   5   4   3

Contents

Dedication to my "doctors"

Doctor (Dr.) from Latin, teacher, *docere,* to teach

Dedicated to the many people who all through my life have
offered a hand, inspired me, pointed a way.
Dedicated especially to those creative, prepared teachers
who labored to fulfill the high office of helping-and-
teaching, and loved it—people in my life like Dr. Frank
Reilly, Dr. Bernard Klonis, Dr. Lajos Egri, Dr. Irving Lee,
Dr. Wendell Johnson, Dr. Ernie Jones. And to Dr. Marie
Beynon Ray, who taught me "how never to be tired."
I kneel to them. To me, they are all doctors.

Session 1   *Feeling and the easiest watercolor method*

Easy way to begin your painting

Your feeling

Easier to learn watercolor *the new creative way*

What a painting *is* and *is not*

[1]

[2]

To me, watercolor is the most exciting, satisfying way to paint. It's the cleanest, freshest, and fastest. And working with painters over the years, I have developed *new ways to make watercolor easy to handle, easy to learn*. In addition I have learned to feel and shape my feeling in my painting. In the next few pages I touch on (1) a sure way to get your painting started, and (2) a few simple ways to handle water, brush, paint, air. From there we'll get at the work sessions, from the first step right on through.

Your first mark starts you right. This is the beginning of a painting (along the Wildcat River, Jackson, New Hampshire). My first step to a painting is not painting at all. I start with a scribble sketch that takes only a few minutes. A very rough scribble helps me find my feeling and begin to shape it. I use a pencil or a pen or even a nylon-nib pen. Anyone can do a scribble sketch, no drawing skill required. These first marks stand for a couple of trees.

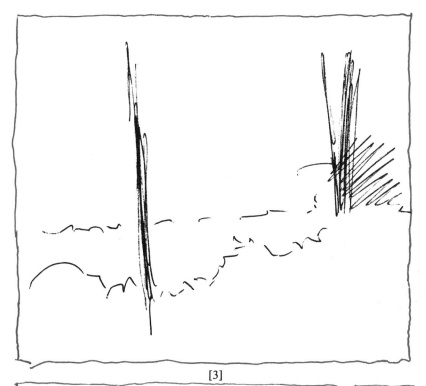

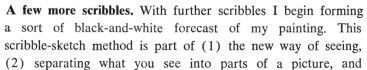

A few more scribbles. With further scribbles I begin forming a sort of black-and-white forecast of my painting. This scribble-sketch method is part of (1) the new way of seeing, (2) separating what you see into parts of a picture, and (3) then arranging the parts your own personal way.

Progressing. The whole sketch is usually a matter of five minutes of seeing and roughing in mass areas. Before I developed the preview scribble sketch, I seldom knew what I had in mind for my painting or what I was going to do with it, until I had struggled my way through the finished painting. I wasted many finished paintings and made frustration the name of the game. I wouldn't think of starting a painting without making a scribble sketch first. In the next chapter I'm doing some scribble sketches for you in detail.

[5]

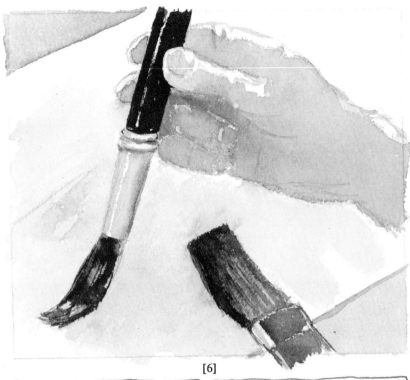

[6]

Water is a magic element in watercolor painting, but it's no mystery. Take a minute to see how to use water, and see some of the distinctive effects you can get with it. No art talent is involved in using water properly. If you have a brush handy and a tube of watercolor paint, try it with me, and you can find out for yourself the secrets of controlling water and making it work for you. I will quickly go through some of the techniques I use all the time.

✳**1 easy procedure: pre-wetting.** A basic technique in my way of watercolor is *spotwetting—washing some plain water onto an area of the paper,* no paint on the brush. I'm doing it here with a very little light gray in the water so that you can see the wetting better against the plain white paper. Wet your brush and move it quickly back and forth across the desired area. Do it lightly and quickly—don't keep going over it. *Then drop that brush.* The brush can be a round or a flat, so long as it's big enough to hold lots of water.

[7]

MOIST, LIVE PAINT RIGHT FROM THE TUBE

"SQUEEZED-DRY" BRUSH

BLACK

[8]

❋2 easy procedure: a dryer brush. This is another basic technique and *the most useful idea you can learn*. You get rid of much of the water from your wet brush by a gentle "squeeze" between your fingers. Why a dryer brush before you touch it to paint? Because you already have the water on the paper, and too much water makes a mess of the painting. What you need on your brush is not more water but some *moist, live paint out of the tube*. You learn water control quickly, and it shows up in your painting.

Excess water on the brush dilutes the paint, turns an intended dark gray into a washed-out light gray. Dip the dryer, reshaped brush into the pure moist paint and let it pick up a little of it. Learn to do that very simple thing, and you've got a major technique going for you.

[9]

[10]

Live paint hits wet surface. You can do this only with paint out of the tube, *not dried pats or cakes of paint.* I am showing what happens in two stages. I have begun to swish that loaded brush on the wet surface, and this is a stop-shot so you can see how it looks at moment of contact. The paint will spread much more as the receptive water picks it up and moves it around. *Try this yourself a few times.*

Paint-and-water work for you. This is what has happened in the few moments since live paint hit the water-wet surface. This "free distribution" is one of the many possible interesting effects to come from paint-and-water. Applying moist paint into wet surface is the second of the simple and easy procedures yet *it's a major technique that is part of the charm of watercolor.* I'll demonstrate it as we go, and you can do it many more ways.

6

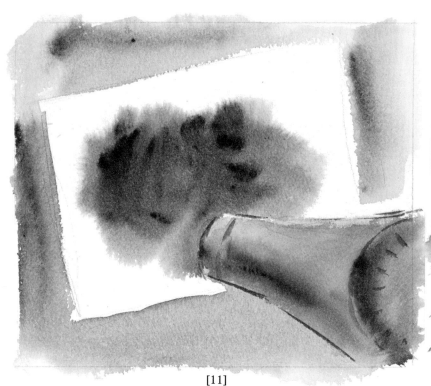

[11]

[12]

✳**3 easy procedure: drying as a "must."** I am putting a hair dryer onto the paper just to demonstrate that air is one of your major control elements to successful watercolor painting. Outdoors of course you let your paper dry by itself, usually a matter of a few minutes. To speed things up indoors—especially on damp days—I use a hair dryer. It's a perfectly legitimate watercolor tool and very useful to me. But you certainly can get along without one.

See that it's dry. You can see whether your paper is dry by turning it toward the light and looking for wet reflection. Touch your hand to it to make sure. Stopping for a few minutes to let your paper dry is one of the top secrets and main techniques of watercolor painting. Further along, I will create for you a disaster or two from painting into wet areas when I should be letting them dry.

7

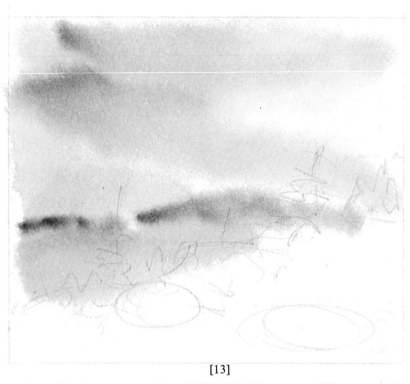

[13]

[14]

So with those three steps—(1) pre-wetting, (2) applying moist tube paint into the pre-wet, and (3) stopping to let the paper dry at routine moments—you can see you'd be able to get a lot going in a painting without knowing much more. We'll build on that three-way basic technique, each a creative act.

The above represents a first wash-in and a first drying period. Schoodic Peninsula, Maine, Frenchman's Bay.

man's Bay.

Two simple, creative acts. As with the handling of water and air, almost all the creative acts in this system of watercolor painting involve plain judgment rather than special skills. For example, brush selection, getting the most useful types and sizes of brushes. Even paper selection is a creative decision that helps you develop your watercolor skills most readily. The most skilled of artists can't make up for a "wrong" paper. In Session 10, I am specific about paper and brushes.

[15]

[16]

Stop and do the step. Schoodic finished. In doing a painting like this before a painting class, I like to demonstrate one step at a time, stop each time, and let the painters do it. They enjoy the demonstration more, and there's no surer way to develop watercolor skills than to do an unfamiliar bit after seeing it demonstrated. Doing it yourself does something for your brain-and-fingers. And of course catching onto one step makes the next one that much easier. Keep your paints handy!

Sometimes pre-wetting, sometimes not. Much of the time you'll run into the situation where it's better to put the paint-and-water down *without pre-wetting the surface.* I'll prepare you for that ahead of time. It's just as easy to do as the pre-wet way, and it calls for pretty much the same sort of stroking, no problem. It's one more easy and related technique variety you'll pick up and have ready to use.

9

[17]

[18]

"Skip-brushing." With a small change in wetting and brush conditions (like the squeezed brush—Frame 7), you'll do single-stroke special effects in "skip-brushing." Such effects as pebbles on a beach, bark on a tree, leaves on the ground, a hundred different "patterns." Each exciting stage of technical mastery is not a matter of having special aptitudes but in learning how to apply the few simple techniques like (1) the skip-brush, (2) the pre-wet stroke, (3) the no-pre-wet stroke —and deciding which one to use to suit a situation.

Simple options = the new creativity. Such options as more water, less water. Dry it, don't dry it now. More paint, less paint. A wetter stroke or a dryer stroke. A slow stroke, a fast stroke. Really simple decisions like those. That's about all there is to putting paint down onto paper. We'll go over each in turn so you may quickly master that part of painting. Knowing the routine options, and being able each time to decide which technique to use—not fumbling around—is the good road to fresh and exciting paintings.

10

[19]

[20]

Note that thus far, though I talk of your becoming a master craftsman, I have called for "no talent," no special kind of skills. The talent you need is (1) desire to paint, (2) interest enough to give it some of your time and attention, and (3) a decent try. Now before we go any further handling paint, I'd like you to think about something that transcends brushwork, something even more useful to you: How to get feeling into your painting. *It is only through feeling that you can fulfill yourself as a creative artist.*

Feeling. The simplest and most useful thing about painting is something that not one in ten painters knows much about. When you look into yourself, you find you have feelings about nearly everything around you: It'd be pretty hard for you to want to paint anything *without* having a feeling about it. But sometimes the feeling suffocates because a painter is not prepared to cultivate it. Feeling is beginning here in this picture. And it accelerates to a high point in Frame 21.

11

[21]

[22]

Creative painting is easier to learn. I'll show you how to recognize what you feel about something you'd like to paint, how to develop it, and how to shape that feeling into watercolor paintings so others may share your feeling—as here. *You can learn faster to paint with feeling than without—* once you hook up your seeing to your feeling. You will find out quickly what your feeling is. Secondly, the new way, you will know how to give it shape in progressive easy steps.

A painting is something else. For a moment stop thinking of doing a painting, and instead think with me what a watercolor painting "is" and what it "is not." *This is the hardest bit of thinking for any painter to learn, beginner or not.* A painting "is," in one respect, a flat surface, maybe 22 by 15 inches, on which you make some marks with paint and water. A painting is not the tall trees and wet water and hard rocks out there, nor anything like them.

12

[23]

[24]

A painting is less and more. A painting is not the same thing as the magnolia blossoms I see next to our driveway nor can I ever make it so. My painting and yours is *less* than the trees you can climb or the flowers you can feel and smell. Yet at the same time that our painting *is less,* it is also *more.* But above all, it is nothing like "reality." *It's something else.* This is true of "reminiscent" subject matter and the "no subject" paintings. Equally.

You can't put the tree in. I've been demonstrating to artist audiences an obvious bit of information—that you can't put the thing itself into your painting—like a ten-ton tree with a thousand branches and 500,000 leaves. Or even if the tree had only 219 leaves, you still couldn't put a tree with its 219 leaves into your painting. People "believe" me when I say that, but they paint as though they didn't.

[25]

[26]

You can't put a million tons of water in. You step on those solid rocks and you feel the ocean spray on your face, and you're inspired to get the rocks and the ocean and the action into your painting. You can't put millions of tons of ocean and rocks into your flat picture that measures 22 inches by 15, and weighs maybe an ounce. If you can't put into your picture the physical thing itself, then *you have two main alternatives.*

Alternative 1—the junk painting. You can try to imitate what's out there—try to copy it—and end up with a painted inventory of something. I suppose a computer could give us such a junk inventory, or a kid with a camera could use up a roll of film doing it. Whatever else a picture postcard copy of something may be, it's not much of a product of your creative mind, nor can I ever think of it as a work of art. Besides, it's harder to do than a creative work because when I am "copying" I'm fumbling along without feeling and inspiration.

14

[27]

[28]

Alternative 2—Your own thing. Since you can't get the rocks themselves into your painting and you're not satisfied to do a paper imitation of something real, why not do something you can do well? *Do your own thing.* Feel those rocks and the surf in their tense encounter as it all appears to you, and create a painting of your feeling about it. Paint it so someone else may feel it somewhat the way you do. Like an actor feeling a role and interpreting it for an audience.

Another day, a different painting (Mood #2). And tomorrow at the same place when the weather's different, and the hour's different, and you feel different, paint a different feeling into your painting. This is Boothbay, Maine, after the storm. In a new season, go back to Boothbay and feel it again, and paint it as you feel it then. The setting turns your feeling on, and you respond. *I think some such feeling accompanies all creativity.*

15

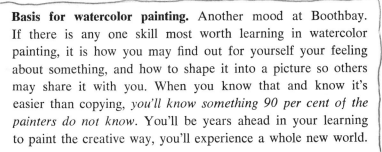

[29]

[30]

Basis for watercolor painting. Another mood at Boothbay. If there is any one skill most worth learning in watercolor painting, it is how you may find out for yourself your feeling about something, and how to shape it into a picture so others may share it with you. When you know that and know it's easier than copying, *you'll know something 90 per cent of the painters do not know.* You'll be years ahead in your learning to paint the creative way, you'll experience a whole new world.

Ecstasy of feeling. When you paint your feeling, two of the sublimest things happen to you: You experience the glow of having felt deeply about something. That's rare enough. But far more lavish is the second feeling that comes over you while you are exercising your creative faculties—the ecstasy of creative power, the feeling of putting together. That is the feeling that shows in your painting.

16

[31]

[32]

My painting is me. I said the painting is something less than reality and at the same time something more. Not an imitation of anything, it is its own thing. To me, *my painting is me.* It is my own thing. It is my successor to the thing I painted from. And when I hang it in my living room—or someone else likes it and buys it from me—it's a picture not of a place or a thing but of something I have felt. *It's a moment in my life that I can't ever experience again.* It's me living.

The one big "how" of painting. Are you ready to begin a sketch? This next session is a technique I have developed helping myself and other struggling artists. If any one of my sessions could be considered the one big "how" of painting, I think Session 2 coming up would have to be it. It is the key to developing one's creative powers, and at the same time it shows how natural and easy creative painting can be. *Once you become a creative painter, you'll want to paint forever.*

17

How you "find" your feeling and make paintable subjects

How you discover the Creative Compartment, and come up with things
you never dreamed of

The most useful sketching method in creative art

[33]

[34]

You begin to be different from the non-painting public the moment you stop to look and ask yourself: What is it about this thing that makes me stop and "feel" about it? And makes me want to paint a picture . . .

Cup your hands to look through, or use a viewfinder—it helps you "frame" something out there. It shuts out everything but what you want to think about for a painting.

A "viewfinder" is a small piece of paper or cardboard (six inches by four is about right) cut out to form a frame opening to look through. Hold it six to twelve inches from your eyes, and look through it with half-closed eyes. Half-shut eyes diffuse the detail, and let you see what's out there more as abstract, mass areas that you will be concerned with. This half-closing of the eyes has served me all my painting life.

19

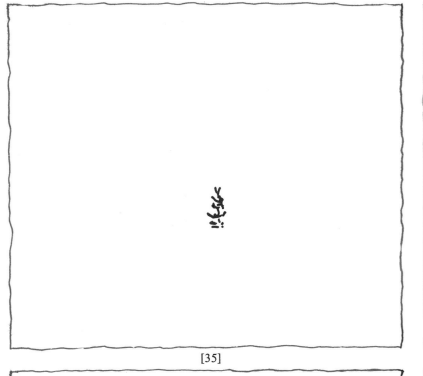

[35]

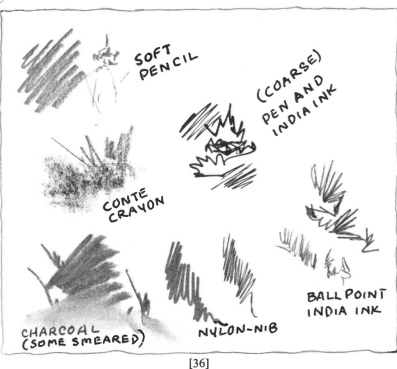

[36]

The one most useful mark you can make. On your layout pad, scribble something that appears especially interesting out there—like one of the highest conifer trees. This is the single most useful act—it starts me creating my watercolor painting. I like the 11 by 14 or 14 by 17 pad, thirty to fifty sheets to the pad, with a supporting cardboard backing. It's easy to carry and use. And I like semi-opaque paper with a slightly textured surface that takes pencil, charcoal, conté crayon, or ink. Art-supply stores or art departments have them.

Anything will do to scribble with. A soft pencil—2-b, 3-b, not anything harder. Conté crayon is fine, it smears less than charcoal (which needs to be sprayed with fixative). Pen-and-ink is good, so are the ball-point black-ink pens (I like a broad one). The modern nylon-nibbed black-ink pen serves very well for the fast scribble sketch. In my scribble sketches reproduced in this book, some are ball-point pen, some nylon-nibbed. I like charcoal too, in spite of its messiness. Experiment, see what you like.

[37]

[38]

What's a scribble sketch? "Scribble" is what my grandson Scott called it when he was six. He scribbles on his pad to form shapes. He hasn't needed any training for scribbling as such, and I guess no one else does. Scribbling comes natural. By the minute, you get more confident with it. My other grandson, Dale, when he was six sketched what he saw while waiting for his father at the airport, using the scribble technique.

Any kind of scribble is OK. I don't want to make a big thing of how to scribble. My way is to put the nylon-nibbed pen onto the paper, move it about to fill in something to represent a shape, as I have done here. Any style will do. Your scribble doesn't have to look like a tree. Whatever you put down, it is only your present scribble symbol for a tree shape. I suggest a *firm* scribble, about as demonstrated here (just as easy firm). Practice a few scribbles of things around you—on any piece of paper, even discarded newspaper.

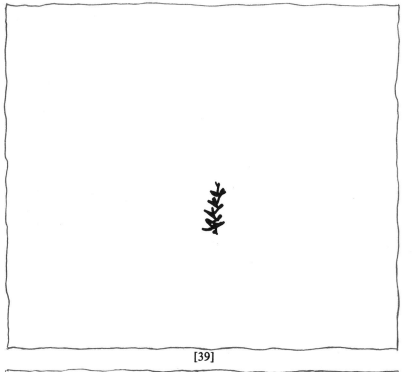

[39]

[40]

Leave yourself space. Where on your pad do you place the conifer tree scribble? Place it near the middle, and relatively small. This leaves space for the other things you will sketch around this tree. And leave some airspace around the whole sketch. Putting the tree in the center here doesn't mean it will be in the center in your finished picture. Placement of a top-interest item in your picture is an art in itself, and you'll presently see how easy it is to become expert at it.

Beginning your first mass shape. To go with the tree as accessory and to form a mass shape, scribble in some of the trees near it, to form an upper boundary to this section. Let the ridge swerve down to the left into a sort of valley. As you see, the sketching here isn't anything much to do—it's largely a matter of scribbling with dark lines—no detail, no attempt to "draw." Forget drawing.

[41]

[42]

One whole major mass. This is the same ridge filled in as a single mass unit. Keeping your pen continuously on the paper, scribble your pen around to form a fill-in, not at all a detailed drawing. Even a circular continuous motion. Mine is just a scribble, and it could be much cruder and still serve the purpose of getting something on paper to look at. It's easiest when you do it in steps as I do here. Viewfinder or cupping hands, do your looking with half-shut, squinted eyes.

A minor mass area. A second ridge farther away seems to belong in this shot. Scribble it in as a single area only half as wide as the front ridge, and a little lighter—a contrast to suggest that the area is less important, and farther away. Things farther away usually appear smaller, lighter, less colorful, or fuzzier. You could feel you have a thousand trees and bushes but you're better off thinking of this total picture thus far in terms of painting: two areas, the smaller one medium gray and the other darker.

[43]

[44]

Mass area ⚹3. I have scribbled in with light lines an indication of the foreground. At the right it's near us, and at the left it runs off into the distance. Now that I have something that looks like the beginning of a picture, I want to pause a moment and show a little about light-and-dark tones in watercolor painting, and how to indicate them easily in the scribble sketch. *Contrasting light and dark tones are pretty much the story of all painting but especially watercolor.*

The whole range of tones. You could have scribbled your sections this rough or still rougher, and you'd still have the essence of a painting. That's because you've made each section into a shape that contrasts with all the others: ⚹1 in the frame is a light gray; ⚹2 a middle gray; ⚹3 is dark gray. And the sky ⚹4 is white. *Those four tones plus black are the entire tone range in scribble-sketching and watercolor painting.* The in-between tones are hardly worth thinking about ever, certainly not now.

24

[45]

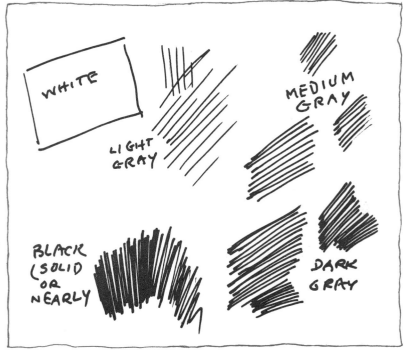

[46]

Think in 5 tones, from white to black. It is vital to your sketch technique that in this structural stage you *scribble not in color but in the five tones—black, grays, white.* Color at this time can only dazzle and keep you from developing more fundamental skills. Stay with the five tones and we'll take on color when you can do it as a transitional step, and accept that the hundreds of colors fall into five tones too.

How you do the 5 tones (also called "values"). For white, it's the paper itself, little or no stroking on it. For light gray, scribble in fewer strokes, wider apart, or thinner than for a darker gray. Middle gray, the strokes are closer together or wider strokes. And still closer together for dark gray. For near-black your strokes are almost solid. Any which way, any direction, straight or circular, so long as you get the desired tone-depth (degree of dark-lightness).

[47]

[48]

Kill a picture with one mass. I have put in a middle-tone scribble to show you a way to ruin the picture. The middle gray stands for deep blue sky on a clear day. This middle-tone sky is the beginning of making your picture a *junk view* or an unthought-out inventory of what seems to be in sight, but not the shaping of your feeling about this scene. Also this junk way the picture has no one strong contrast area for the viewer's eyes—no focal point, no high interest point. A real nothing.

"But that's the way the view is," someone says. Right. But you are supposed to paint not what's "there," not an inventory, not a copy, but how you feel about it. That big tree has something to do with your Big Feeling, and we are at the crossroads. Something has to happen here. We have to make a decision. At this point it may be useful to learn a trick the top creative artists use when they want to change the sketch and not sacrifice the good work they've already done.

26

[49]

[50]

Changing your sketch most easily. I remind you I said the pad was semi-opaque, which of course means also semi-transparent. You can slip your present scribble sketch under a fresh sheet on your 10 by 14 pad and quickly do a fresh new sketch over the old one, changing it as you intend. In this new sketch I want to retain everything but that solid blue-gray sky. So through the semi-transparent sheet I sketch (trace) the parts I want to retain.

2 major contrasting masses. I have scribble-sketched a light gray sky everywhere but where I want white clouds. (Remember in sketching and in watercolor painting your whites are supplied by leaving the white paper blank.) I have made the white clouds break behind some of the big trees including the main tree—to make them stand out. We are getting nearer to making our feeling, our big idea, catch fire and *happen*.

27

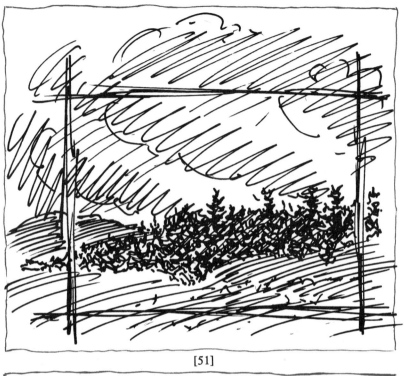

[51]

[52]

Borders affect the picture. These trial borders put my main-interest tree directly in the center of the picture, and also take in several more big trees against the sky to compete with the ⌗1 tree. This arrangement, although carrying high contrast, scatters my "concentrated" point of interest over too big an area. I'll show you what placing your borders can do to improve this picture. *Border placement is one of the most useful techniques you can be master of.*

I try to find one border first. As you see, I have cut off two of the offending trees, gotten them out of the way. This now makes *my main big tree the only one silhouetted against the white cloud.* The other big tree is against gray and thus it contrasts secondary to my main tree. I am not stating any "rules" on this because I want your mind to see me do it a few more times. When you do it yourself, your brain-and-hand develop their own feel for it. Feel for these things comes with doing them enough times, not first learning rules.

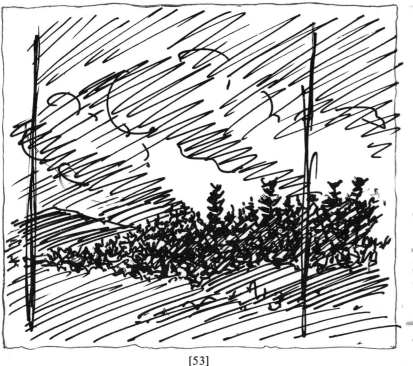

[53]

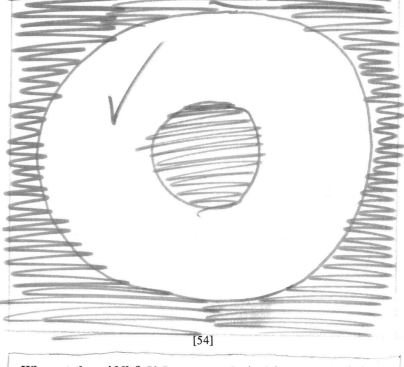

[54]

Second border functional too. I'd like to hold onto most of the far gray hill area at the left, since it seems to be very much a part of my original feeling about this scene. Of course also I need to hold much of that at the left or I'd have very little picture left. So I place my left border without more question. Another reason for putting the border where I have is that it keeps my main tree *away from the middle.*

Why not the middle? If I put my principal interest or climax too close to centerish, the equidistant surrounding areas just about force me to use only small shapes, tending toward monotonous symmetry. On the other hand, if I place the major interest point somewhere between the center and the edges (area check-marked in my diagram), I am providing myself space for larger runs and shapes as well as the small—to lead my viewers more readily to the secondary points of interest. Try both ways, see what works for you.

[55]

[56]

Eliminates the non-functional. In my sketch there's not much happening down low. So I can afford to put the bottom border where it is and block out the wasteland. Good pictures, like effective language, are somewhat a matter of pruning and eliminating—discarding the fat cats. *A tip:* You don't *just think* about where to put your border. Rough a border in (thinking while you do it) and see how it looks. Touching your pen to paper can stimulate your thinking and give you something to evaluate.

Automatic border. The placement of the last borderline is dictated by proportion. However, if I found that the last borderline didn't belong there, I'd start all over again placing my borders. This device of placing your borders is one of the most creative things you can do in shaping your feeling and making your pictures happen. You become proficient at it by facing the problem often, and each time taking a stab at it. You learn it into yourself by doing it.

[57]

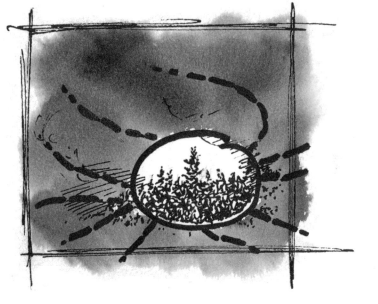

[58]

The miracle of communicating your feeling. At last, your big feeling—climaxed by the dark tree against the white cloud (enlarged here). *This is what the viewer sees first.* From there the eye goes on a beautiful journey of discovery, taking in your initial feeling of a bright day, the cool color, the graceful swing of the mountain ridges, the Maine woods, and the conifer trees reaching up. A miracle of sharing a piece of Maine with your viewers—through a 22 by 15 watercolor, a piece of paper you have painted.

You control the viewer. Can the artist move a viewer's eyes? Neither your picture nor anything in it "moves." But what you do with the areas of your picture can cause the human eye to move—to be attracted first to your major interest area, the high point of your feeling as artist—and from there take journeys back and forth all over the picture, to experience more and more of your feeling. The thousands of tests of eye movements —scientifically done and reported—tell us for sure that that is what happens.

31

Take
your
choice

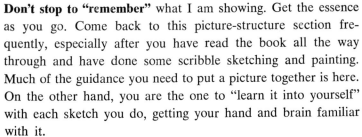

[59]

[60]

Don't stop to "remember" what I am showing. Get the essence as you go. Come back to this picture-structure section frequently, especially after you have read the book all the way through and have done some scribble sketching and painting. Much of the guidance you need to put a picture together is here. On the other hand, you are the one to "learn it into yourself" with each sketch you do, getting your hand and brain familiar with it.

Watercolor version of scribble sketch. This is Saddleback in the Rangeley Mountains area of Maine, on the Appalachian trail. As you recognize, this is the picture for which I've been doing the scribble sketches. Here I have done it for you in black-gray-white watercolor, purposely not in color so that you may check back and compare these watercolor tones with the scribble-sketch tones.

For full-color comparison, see Frame 121, facing page 64.

In the image: LIGHT GRAY, WHITE OF THE PAPER, MIDDLE GRAY, MIDDLE GRAY, LIGHT GRAY, SHARPEST CONTRAST WHITE PAPER, BLACK, MIDDLE GRAY, DARK GRAY, LIGHT GRAY

[61]

[62]

Watercolor paint is transparent, and white paper is a big part of the painting. In all tones—light or dark and full color or black-and-white—the paper shows through the paint and becomes part of the tone. Pure whites, such as the light on the clouds here, are done not with white paint but by leaving those parts of the white paper unpainted. This is quite different from opaque painting such as oil. Traditionally, white paint has no place on the watercolor painter's palette.

Handling other situations via scribble sketch. Now that we've done a step-by-step scribble sketch of dark trees against light sky, I want to demonstrate what's to be done with light against light. And what you can do if you change your mind and get a different feeling halfway through your scribble sketch or even after you've finished it.

33

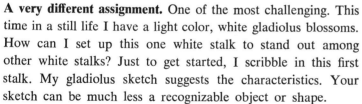

[63]

[64]

A very different assignment. One of the most challenging. This time in a still life I have a light color, white gladiolus blossoms. How can I set up this one white stalk to stand out among other white stalks? Just to get started, I scribble in this first stalk. My gladiolus sketch suggests the characteristics. Your sketch can be much less a recognizable object or shape.

On our way to a junk picture. We could make a whole picture of the one glad but the assignment is for a bouquet, and so I have moved ⚹1 glad to the left and thrown in a few more white blossoms. Their light tone competes with the first glad of course. No one flower stands out, there's nowhere for the eye to begin, and nowhere and everywhere to go. That's the formula for a nothing picture. We are just piling up an inventory of glads and heading toward a seed-catalog picture.

[65]

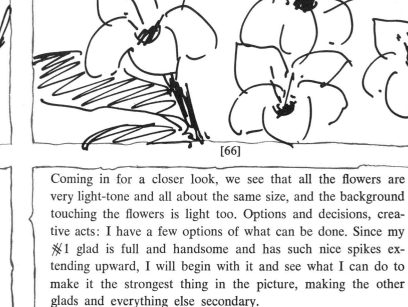

[66]

Compounding our problem. I have put in some leaves to complete an informal flower arrangement for a painting, before facing up to the big problem—how to set up our sketch so we'll have some kind of interesting picture leading to a high point of interest. Note that here as in all scribble sketching, our thinking is in terms of the five tones that come from a black pen. My picture has to "happen" in the sketch or it won't in the finished painting.

Coming in for a closer look, we see that all the flowers are very light-tone and all about the same size, and the background touching the flowers is light too. Options and decisions, creative acts: I have a few options of what can be done. Since my ⧣1 glad is full and handsome and has such nice spikes extending upward, I will begin with it and see what I can do to make it the strongest thing in the picture, making the other glads and everything else secondary.

35

[67]

[68]

I have created a patch of dark background that I need.
I have put it against my ✕1 glad section, and maybe I am on my way to getting the big focal point I've been looking for. Is that a legitimate way to paint? It is the only way I know to paint. You remember in the conifer picture I had to find a white cloud as an element to make my Big Tree stand out. One of the biggest skills you can develop in indoor painting is to create your own backgrounds to suit your purpose. And in the precise tone you need.

I create more helpers. A light-gray shadow-tone on parts of the other flowers holds them back—further keeps them from detracting from my ✕1 glad. A spike leaf in front of the lower-right-hand glad makes that glad less prominent, less competitive. The bright light retained on my ✕1 glad makes it the queen of the picture. It is the first thing the viewer is compelled to see. It typifies all the glads here, and the rest falls into secondary points of interest, completing the picture and expressing my feeling.

[69]

[70]

"Turning yourself on." When I'm sketching the model, I like to begin my sketch the way I begin an outdoor sketch or a still-life subject. I think about what's in front of me that I can see. What do I feel about her and how she looks at this special moment? What could be my principal point of interest? I like the way she has done her hair, and that perky red ribbon. I am ready to rough in an area to represent her head. As my pen touches paper, something very exciting happens.

Pen-to-paper sets me off. For one thing, I have made a start, which for many painters is often a problem. Secondly, getting the head roughed in as a probable high-interest point releases my mind to consider further ideas about the subject. This act of touching pen to paper turns on a compartment of the brain that I have come to call the "Creativity Compartment." Your Creativity Compartment gets into the act and begins to function for you independent of your surface thinking power.

37

[71]

[72]

The sketch moves forward. Looking at the head I have done, my Creativity Compartment comes up with a strong light behind her on the right side where the ribbon is—as in the sketch. Artists are not the only ones to have ideas come to them, seemingly out of the air. It happens to scientists, writers, executives, housewives, doctors, teachers, anyone. Sometimes even after the work is put aside ideas pop up from the Creativity Compartment. Countless times during this book I have bounced out of my sleep with "answers."

Your hand and your brain. A thing to know about this extra creative help is that *your initial thinking combining with your hand at work on your pad* makes a start and tells your super Creativity Compartment that you're not fooling, and any ideas forthcoming will be gratefully received. My scribble sketch proceeds. I extend my lightest light area behind the model's right side which now had better take on the darkest shadow in the picture.

38

[73]

[74]

Suppose your feeling changes during your picture? In the process of shaping your feeling you may come up with a new approach. My sketch here shows a shift of the principal interest area to the left side. Sometimes the new idea occurs while you are finishing your painting or even after. I am grateful for a better idea any time, and I don't hesitate to start over again, see how I come out with the new feeling.

Little things that attract you. The thing that stops you in the beginning and makes you want to paint could be something as unsensational as the highlights on the bark of a tree trunk, a pattern of lobster boats, or the way a model slips into position. Or clouds in formation. To me, *paintings are feelings—usually intimate feelings—made visual.* Just as music may be thought of as feeling shaped in sound.

[75]

[76]

Here I couldn't make up my mind what the one big thing was. When you are seeking watercolor subjects, a good attitude is to turn down complicated shots like this one. Skip the vast heroic Hudson River kind of thing, the elusive Grand Canyon, the scattered jewels of the lake setting at Yosemite. Or the historic signing of the Declaration of Independence or Napoleon rampant at Waterloo. Generally they're too multi to make happen in watercolor.

Feeling a lot about a little. It is more in keeping with modern thinking to close in on one of the many sights around you. Like at Sagamore Hill (Theodore Roosevelt's shrine, Oyster Bay, Long Island, New York). Out of the whole park of sunlit fall foliage and majestic trees, I selected one small maple and one part of the tree's banks of red leaves-in-the-sun. The rustic fence, so typical on Long Island, was, I found, a part of my feeling. In watercolor painting, I like to *make much of little rather than little of much.*

40

[77]

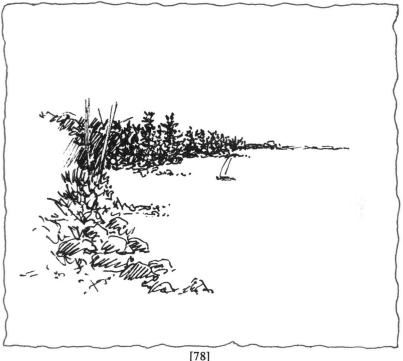

[78]

Your subject is where you feel it. The trick is to find your painting in one of nature's intimacies. I used to look for miles and days to find a "suitable" subject. With experience, I have found many subjects around our house at Manhasset, and at a cottage at Kettle Cove, Sebago Lake, Maine. Each time we go back to the Mount Washington, New Hampshire, base area (this sketch) still another view presents itself to me, begging to be sketched.

By-product of your scribble sketching. Purely as a by-product from scribble sketching, I have developed the freeform pen drawing (two preceding frames and these next ones). You may find your scribble sketching turning in this direction too. I start the freeform pen sketch as I do the scribble sketch— beginning with the principal interest item, adding sections as I feel them. I never know really where a sketch is going when I start but I am learning to stop as soon as I have something simply suggestive.

41

[79]

[80]

Free-and-easy. I do not let myself become careful in this kind of freeform stroking. Let it be free as stroking, and appear as something loose and spontaneous on the page. I try to do subjects small on a 9 by 12 sketch page, allowing plenty of white space; seldom larger. You leave them raw-edged, no border, that's part of their charm. Picture here is same shot as Frame 78 but this time my feeling was for the rocks and trees in foreground.

Similar to watercolor. Sketches like these develop your capacity to handle not just the pen but also watercolor. You develop your capacity for getting a deft start on a picture, and to carry it just so far so the whole picture becomes the shape of your feeling. With no overworking. And, secondly, leaving the uncovered white paper for highlights is precisely what you do in watercolor, and that's another reason for doing plenty of these pen-line sketches.

Symbol of Los Angeles Zoo, Griffith Park, California.

[81]

[82]

Keep the pen going. Be flamboyant about these sketches, as quite obviously I have been with this one, done at Jackson, New Hampshire. Two men stepped into what I was going to sketch, and as they did I asked them to hold it a couple of minutes. Which they did. I liked my moment of rapid whirling with almost continuous nylon-nibbed pen stroking while two high-powered executives on vacation "held it" for me.

Minute sketches. Any place where people are wandering around—at the beaches, lakes, the Maine rocks—you can get quick-sketch practice. Sometimes all you have is ten seconds before the person moves. Leave a sketch unfinished if you must—it could be one of your most spontaneous. When I'm doing figure quickies, I do many separate studies to the page.

[83]

[84]

Bonus assignment, a way to learn sketching: (1) Carry a small sketch notebook, 9 by 12 or smaller, and a black ball-point or a nylon-nibbed pen, and make scribble sketches of all kinds of subjects. Quickies. Not the more finished ones but at first like the earlier ones (Saddleback) in this chapter. Even from the back seat of a car, when necessary, you can work with sketchbook in your lap. Ink sketches for their own sake are fascinating to do, and as you get doing them you'll slip into your own deft style. Save them, show them.

Bonus assignment ⌗2. For practice, do several roughs of the same subject, shifting the feature emphasis as I did in Frames 78 and 79. That's not such an easy thing to do in the beginning but it's amazing what a little conscious practice does for you. Once you catch on to this kind of "seeing"—so you can place your emphasis at will—you're indeed on your way. Sketching is something you can take up for a few moments at a time. Keep filling up your notebook, it records your growing pains, your hits and misses.

44

[85]

[86]

A look back. So far, we have discussed that you do indeed see with feeling, and you can shape your feeling into pictures so viewers may share your feeling. In addition, you can bring your feeling to a peak of interest to attract viewers even before they know precisely what your painting is about. The scribble-sketch way helps you locate your feeling and develop it and put it into effective visual form. *This creative way of painting is easier to learn and gives you more to enjoy than the copycat way.*

A look ahead. Your visual impressions of the world around you, like the world itself, are in color. This next session, Part I of the mini color rough, converts from the five tones of the scribble sketch into the five tones of watercolor, and includes the handling of the brush. If you've never done anything like that before, it could be one of the quiet gratifications of your lifetime.

45

What does the color rough do for you?

Painting in the 5 tones of watercolor

Brush and stroking techniques for the mini rough

[87]

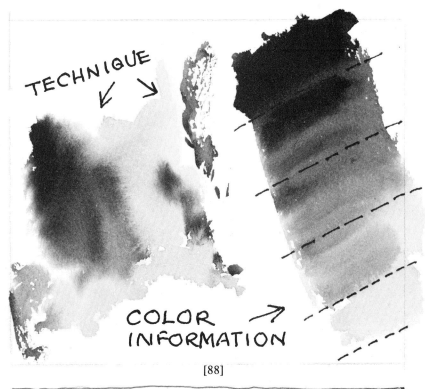

TECHNIQUE

COLOR INFORMATION

[88]

Color tryout. The mini color rough gets you from the pen-and-ink of the scribble sketch into watercolor itself. You do the color tryout half the size of a finish—that small you see it better as a total unit, and with less paper to cover you do it faster and easier. You experiment in this rough state with colors, tones, and contrasts to help you further shape your feeling. Thus by the time you get to your finished painting, you know pretty well what you're about. To me that means fewer failures, more successes.

2 stages make it sure and easy. This is our first full-scale dipping into paint itself. I find the mini color rough is picked up more readily when it is demonstrated in two separate stages: *First stage, as technique*—working the brush, what you do with the water, and getting the moist tube paint going in your rough sketch. *Second stage* sets up the color information needed—for the mini color rough and at the same time for finished watercolor painting.

47

[89]

[90]

(1) **The watercolor technique.** There's no difficulty at all going from pen-and-ink or pencil into watercolor when you do it as I do it here—*work in the five black tones of watercolor as though they were colors*. Of course, once you know the way of watercolor you will do your mini color roughs in full color. (2) *Color*. Thus black is your ✕1 tube. Holding off on color while we do the mini rough in the five tones, we'll slide into color as a major tool when we get into the next session.

Largely color options. The mini color rough does not require a great deal of painting skill. It does, however, confront you with options—the color to use, the tone of it, and the colors to go with it. Once you have the simple color information working for you at your finger tips and the technique of using your paint, the options and your decisions can be a real fun part of painting.

[91]

[92]

A different kind of pencil rough. As in the opening mini rough, I'd like to do a few steps in the Saddleback picture. You are aware of how we began it in the scribble sketch—with the outstanding conifer tree, which we said was our high point of feeling. Beginning with the tree as before, I have not used heavy ink lines but light pencil lines *as guide* for the placement of our watercolor wash areas. In this sketch there is no need for the marked-out areas to match precisely with the scribble sketch.

I use a 15 by 11 size (sometimes smaller), one quarter of a full 30 by 22 *rough surface* watercolor sheet. An H-1 or B-1 pencil won't smear. In the original scribble sketch of Saddleback I used a pen-and-ink light gray for the sky, to represent a light blue. Now I'm in watercolor, and I have washed in a light gray here, to represent the same *light blue sky.* That's the tone of gray it would come to in black-and-white photograph.

49

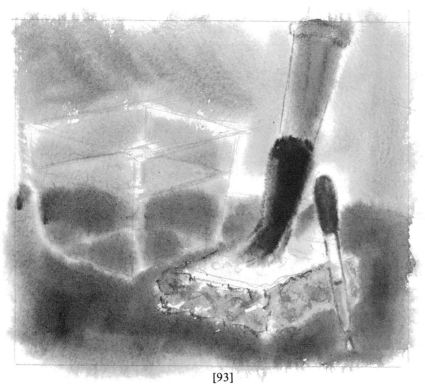

[93]

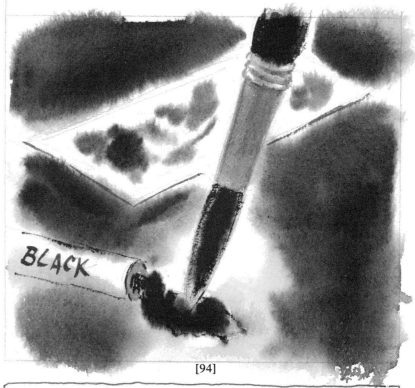

[94]

A brushload of water. A brush picks up more water than needed—and it holds the water like an eyedropper. It's built to do that. It's a good idea to touch the brush to the sponge each time, to drain off some of the excess water. I make it standard practice to dip and drain.

Pickup and tryout. With moderately wet brush, touch it to the moist, thick paint fresh out of the tube, take the brush away with some paint on it. *Touch the brush to your tryout sheet,* so you know what tone to expect when your brush hits your sketch paper. The tryout sheet is also standard practice with me—ever since, during a demonstration, I made it tough on myself by getting some unwanted burnt sienna on my brush and into my painting.

50

[95]

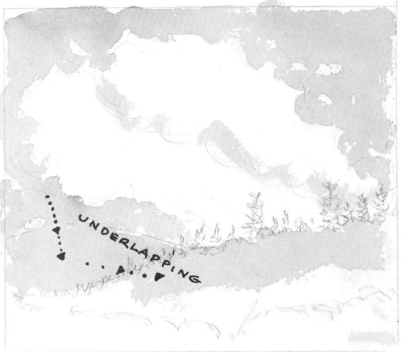

[96]

Fresh, suggestive. Continuing the sketch, you swish your wet brush of paint lightly back and forth onto the *dry sheet,* letting the paint take hold where it happens to. The white flecks of paper show through my gray wash, a desirable effect here. The nature of the mini color rough is (1) suggestive rather than delineative, (2) fresh stroking, not worked-over, and (3) a feeling of unfinish and spontaneity. Sketchy, freeform. *Watercolor paint dries about a tone lighter than it looks wet.*

Second load and underlapping. Your brush runs out of paint. You go back for more water, touch the sponge for drain-off, get more paint, use the tryout sheet, all as before. You resume on your sky area, picking up above the spot where you left off. *Underlapping:* Note that the wash of sky extends over into the two ridge areas. Underlapping like this keeps you from getting "gap-fencing" and "stain-fencing" (both are blemishes that separate areas when you don't want areas separated. We'll go into both in detail later).

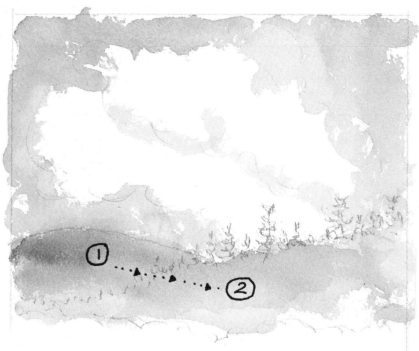

[97]

[98]

Underlapping extended. The underlap of Frame 97 is still wet, and I have washed over it a middle gray for (1) the distant ridge against the light gray sky, as you see. Just a flat, one-tone wash-in, with no delineation, which in turn I have extended to underlap further my (2) foreground main ridge. This sketch, I remind myself, is to set up tones and areas in competition with each other. That means I am painting these areas not as they "are" but as I desire them if I want to make my finished painting *happen*.

For only moderate contrast. We again use our technique of looking through half-shut eyes. This time to get some idea of the relative color-tones of the two ridges. The back ridge appears as the middle-gray tone I need. This background ridge, maybe a mile away, is to *contrast only moderately in tone to the foreground ridge,* which I know from my scribble sketch will be a darker gray tone. Even when we get to full color we'll think in terms of the same five tones.

[99]

[100]

Darkest area in picture. With additional paint on my brush I have saved my darkest tone for this foreground ridge mass area that is so vital to my feeling in the picture. The dark gray, with some splotches of solid black, suggests the necessarily dark foreground conifers to build up my contrast against the clouds. *Laying uneven tones:* When I wash in this dark gray, I turn my brush this way and that—so my tone is laid not even, like a cloudless sky, but *uneven,* to suggest nearness and the irregularity of the tree area.

Brush technique for uneven tones. I said I turn the brush "this way and that." Holding the brush as usual, I revolve my whole hand to the left and then to the right as I move the brush over the surface. This varies the pressure on the brush and causes an irregular release of the water-and-paint from the brush. Up-and-down irregularity in pressure would accomplish something similar. If I hold the brush in one position and work it back and forth across the sheet, I am likely to get more of what I call "flat" or even tones.

53

[101]

[102]

How do you prefer to hold your brush? I like to hold it the way I was taught by the watercolor master Bernard Klonis, as here illustrated. So many times I have seen him demonstrate brush dexterity—by the movement of his wrist or the rolling of the brush in his fingers. Many experienced watercolor painters and brush-lettering people hold the brush this way, and with no more pressure than is needed for holding a pen to write a signature. Try several holds, and use the one that feels freest and you can do most with.

A light-gray mass area. I have washed in the foreground of ※1 ridge (now dry), along with its extension to the left, fading off into the distance. Cloud shadows are in too, a tone darker than the blue sky. I have used light gray to indicate light greens and yellows usually found in foreground bushes and foliage. One thing I don't want in this foreground is massing of dark colors. Dark here would detract from the top of my ※1 ridge. *Reminder about water:* Change it when it gets too dark (usually near the end of a picture).

[103]

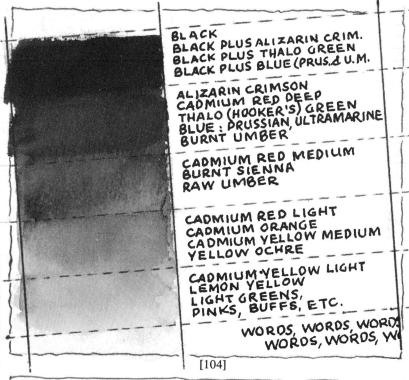

BLACK
BLACK PLUS ALIZARIN CRIM.
BLACK PLUS THALO GREEN
BLACK PLUS BLUE (PRUS. & U.M.

ALIZARIN CRIMSON
CADMIUM RED DEEP
THALO (HOOKER'S) GREEN
BLUE: PRUSSIAN, ULTRAMARINE
BURNT UMBER

CADMIUM RED MEDIUM
BURNT SIENNA
RAW UMBER

CADMIUM RED LIGHT
CADMIUM ORANGE
CADMIUM YELLOW MEDIUM
YELLOW OCHRE

CADMIUM YELLOW LIGHT
LEMON YELLOW
LIGHT GREENS,
PINKS, BUFFS, ETC.

WORDS, WORDS, WORDS
WORDS, WORDS, W

[104]

Surroundings alter impact. To conclude Saddleback for now: The high point of the picture occurs in the contrast of my ✕1 tree against the white cloud behind it (here enlarged), I have used some solid black where that tree touches the white cloud. I have let the paper dry before putting in this overlay of my darkest paint. I have used some of the same deep tone on the other trees within the same area but not against white sky, thus creating in those areas much less contrast, less drama.

Things to come. Meantime as we talk here about tones and colors, don't be too concerned about which tones of gray stand for which colors of the spectrum. In this frame I am listing tones and their equivalent colors—a promise of what is to come in the color chapter to begin after two more frames.

55

[105]

[106]

A look back: from pen to watercolor. We have just converted from the five tones of black pen-and-ink to the same five tones from a single tube of black watercolor paint. In addition, we have said that the five tones of a tube of black watercolor paint are precisely the five tones into which all the colors of the world fit.

A look forward. Now we'll demonstrate color itself in terms of the five tones you are already familiar with.

Color is generally thought of as something mysterious and complicated. And in its total it is. But it doesn't have to be for painters. In the next chapter I am demonstrating only the few simple color ideas I can't paint without—yet all I ever need. With this start, the more you paint and the more you think about color, the more you will build your color resourcefulness.

Session 4   *Your painting comes alive with color*

World of color in 5 tones

Simple keys to color mixing and putting colors together in your paintings

c-o-l-o-r

r-e-d

y-e-l-l-o-w

b-l-u-e

[107]

TOUCH FLESH INTO BACKGROUND

DEEP GREEN ON GARMENT AND BACKGROUND

KEEP COLOR THEME INTEGRATED

[108]

Color is not words. A person blind from birth cannot know what you mean by the word *color*. Nothing you could say would describe a color. That's because "red" and "yellow" and "blue" are not things but *general names for sensations that do not exist outside ourselves,* and that have come to our minds through our eyes, and moreover through chemistry in our eyes. I won't take the space to prove that. You may find it fascinating to read a book or two on light waves and how your eyes function in the process of "seeing" color.

Two kinds of color knowledge. (1) *Mechanical:* This chapter offers color fundamentals—like how to mix colors for painting flesh, hair, shadows, tree trunks, anything at all. And putting colors together in your paintings—for more contrast or less, how to make conflicting colors "go" together, and how to make the same color appear brighter or duller. All easily picked up. (2) *Experience knowledge:* No one can tell you this kind. You get it by painting, and the more you paint the more resourceful you can be with color.

58

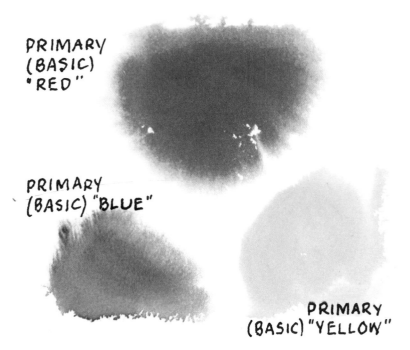

PRIMARY (BASIC) "RED"

PRIMARY (BASIC) "BLUE"

PRIMARY (BASIC) "YELLOW"

[109]

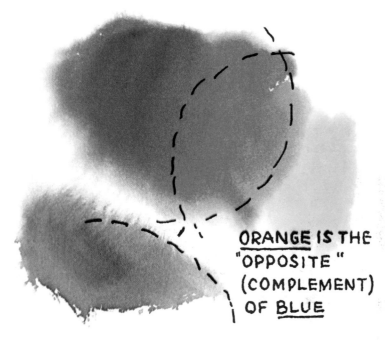

ORANGE IS THE "OPPOSITE" (COMPLEMENT) OF BLUE

[110]

From three basic paint colors I have mixed over a thousand colors, all I would ever need in watercolor painting. (It's useful to know you can do that but it's easier to mix your paint from a basic twelve to fifteen colors.) These three colors are called *primary* because theoretically all other color comes from them, whereas *not one of the three primary colors can be made from any other two colors in the world*. These are not the precise three primaries as the chemist knows them, but they are the nearest I can come from artists' paints.

Making "orange"—a second-generation color. Orange (red-orange) comes from combining primary red and primary yellow. Thus I think of orange as a second-generation color. Colors with yellow or with red are thought of as "warm" colors. *Orange is the complement of blue*—because each supplies in primary color what the other lacks (orange being made of both yellow and red). For now, accept all this as true and useful, as I did when I first heard it. You can know its soundness only as you make colors serve you.

59

GREEN IS THE COMPLEMENT OF RED

[111]

PURPLE IS THE COMPLEMENT OF YELLOW

[112]

"Green" as second-generation color. This is the third in this series of the four (to me) most useful pieces of color information I know of. As you see, primary yellow and primary blue combine to form green—dozens of greens. Colors with a blue influence in them are thought of as "cool." *Green is the complement of primary red*—each primary has a complementary color made up of the remaining two primaries, in this case yellow and blue, to form green.

"Purple" as second-generation color. Primary red and primary blue combine for purple (many purples), and *purple's complement is yellow*. Don't stop to memorize these color frames. Frequent exposure to these pictures, and thinking about them will help get them into your art brain. Nothing hard about learning color but painting in color yourself is the best way to become a color master.

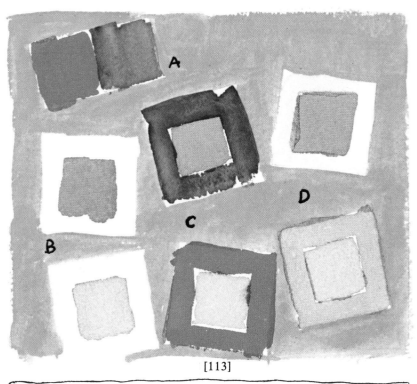

[113]

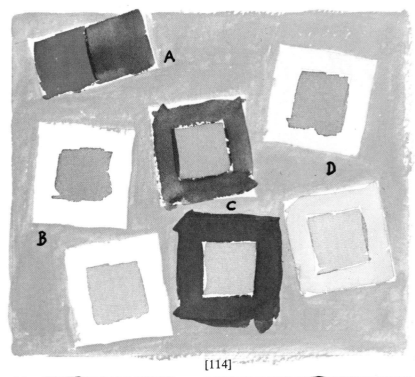

[114]

(a) **Complementary colors,** blue and red-orange, placed together in somewhat equal quantities tend to intensify and fight each other. No color is ever seen alone—thus what surrounds a color affects it. The same light red-orange core appears (b) dull against white paper, (c) brighter and livelier against dark blue, and (d) darkest of all against pale blue. The same light blue-tone core looks (b) duller against white, (c) lighter but overwhelmed by the bright red, and (d) darker against the pale pink setting.

(a) **Primary red and its complement green** together this way attract attention to themselves, and tend to kill your feeling in a painting. Change tone or surroundings, and what happens? The same diluted red core appears (b) dullest against white (paper), (c) "pinker" against dark green, and (d) darker against light green. The diluted light green core looks (b) duller against white, (c) brilliant against deep solid red, and (d) darker against light pink. The white paper you paint on acts as a color.

61

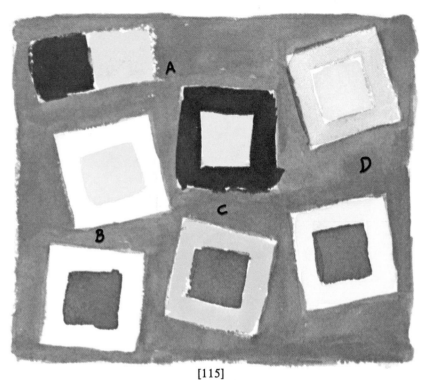

[115]

[116]

Complementaries. (a) Solid purple and solid yellow are seldom used in equal quantities. A light-tone yellow core appears (b) almost lost against white paper, (c) bright and virile against dark purple, (d) deeper and "companionable" against orchid-light purple. A light-tone purple core is something else. The same core seems (b) strong against white, (c) brighter against full-strength yellow, and (d) deeper and vibrant, dominating a light yellow. Change the core tones, and you get still different contrasts.

Contrast of "pure" ungrayed color against its grayed complement. (a) Solid green-blue against light *grayed red*. (b) Light yellow against grayed deep purple. (c) Solid medium red against grayed light blue-green. Any color can be grayed—"neutralized"—in many ways. The two leading ways: 1- By mixing in some of the color's complement, as (d) thalo green and (e) medium red. 2- Adding (f) black (a touch or much) or (g) burnt sienna or burnt umber. Example: (h) medium red+a little black=H-1, or more black=H-2.

62

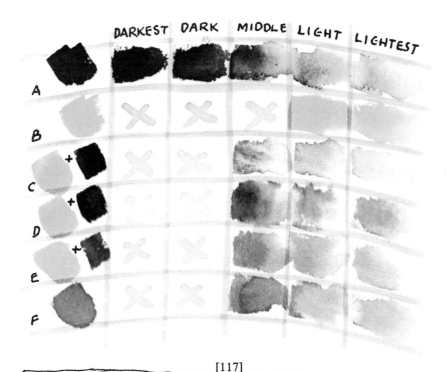

	DARKEST	DARK	MIDDLE	LIGHT	LIGHTEST
A					
B		X	X	X	
C		X	X		
D					
E		X	X		
F		X	X		

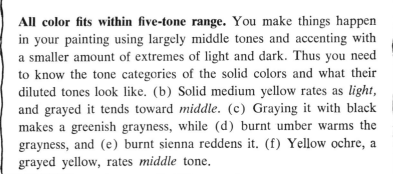

[117]

	DARKEST	DARK	MIDDLE	LIGHT	LIGHTEST
A					
B		X			
C		X	X		
D		X	X	X	
E		X	X	X	
F					

[118]

All color fits within five-tone range. You make things happen in your painting using largely middle tones and accenting with a smaller amount of extremes of light and dark. Thus you need to know the tone categories of the solid colors and what their diluted tones look like. (b) Solid medium yellow rates as *light,* and grayed it tends toward *middle.* (c) Graying it with black makes a greenish grayness, while (d) burnt umber warms the grayness, and (e) burnt sienna reddens it. (f) Yellow ochre, a grayed yellow, rates *middle* tone.

No red is as dense as black (a). Even (b) alizarin crimson and (c) deep red, deep as they seem, rate only *dark,* and in watercolor you use them largely in their lighter tones. (d) Solid medium red classifies as *middle* tone. (e) Light red (red-orange) has a lot of yellow in it, "warm," and full-strength it rates only *light,* as does (f) orange (light red+ yellow). Both orange and light red appear cooler as you water them lighter. You could do without stocking deep red— you make it by adding a touch of alizarin to medium red.

DARKEST DARK MIDDLE LIGHT LIGHTEST

[119]

DARKEST DARK MIDDLE LIGHT LIGHTEST

[120]

Color deepened, grayed, diluted. Each color here begins as its own solid and darkest tone, and note that solid they are about as dense as black. (b) Adding a touch of black (a) makes alizarin crimson a maroon. Black adds density to many deep colors. (c) Alizarin+(d) ultramarine blue=purple. A little more alizarin, a little less . . . and you get delightful colors in the orchid-purple tones. (e) Prussian blue. (f) Gray it with a touch of light red, and I like it still more. For effective use, you either dilute or gray your colors.

Variations in green. See what can happen to one of the basic colors from the tube—(b) thalo green. You seldom use it raw, you deepen it or you may gray it—with (c) black, (d) burnt sienna, sometimes alizarin. For lighter greens, (e) mix thalo with medium yellow for an early-spring green, or (f) mix it with yellow ochre for a more neutral (grayer) kind of green. Thousands of intriguing colors come from mixtures and their (watered-out) tones.

Frame 121: Opposite. Painted on location for these demonstrations. Mount Saddleback area, Rangeley, Maine.

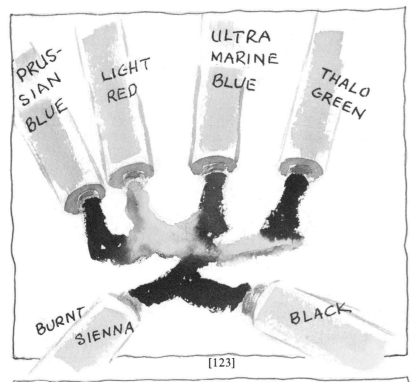

[123]

[124]

Bonus assignment. Nothing can help you more to become good at color than frequent workouts with paint and brush. Do your own experiments or try some of these: *Neutralizing a color.* Try for yourself (1) how a little red changes (a) Prussian blue, (b) ultramarine blue, (c) thalo green (makes an olive). (2) How a little burnt sienna changes those same three colors, and how it affects black. (3) Increase the quantity of burnt sienna for further color effects. Go wild, try neutralizing a whole range of colors.

Bonus assignment, part 2. (1) With informal freeform washes, make a few spots of core of half-strength yellow, surrounded by (a) burnt sienna, (b) maroon. (2) Do the same with core of light-tone spring green surrounded by (a) burnt sienna, (b) deep purple, (c) deep green-black. (3) *Light greens:* Do some (a) thalo green+medium yellow. (b) Thalo green+yellow ochre. Or (c) Prussian blue+medium yellow. (d) For a light cold green: thalo green pure out of tube+ water—middle tone, lightest tone.

Frame 122: Opposite, painting made on-the-spot, Kettle Cove, Sebago Lake, Maine. Demonstrated step-by-step, Session 9.

[125]

[126]

Now that you have had color, I'd like to finish up quickly with the mini color rough as a step in watercolor painting. Non-delineative, unfinished arrangement of color tones—that's what your mini color rough should look like to someone else. To you, it should be that and your tentative color recommendation, a speculation on your part of what color might add up to in your finish. It is putting color to your feeling. A crude thing, it should look like you did it in a few minutes, which indeed you usually do.

This is the place to do your probing. Suppose when you finish your mini color rough you're not satisfied with it—it got away from you. *That's the moment for rethinking and another try at it.* As here at Jackson, New Hampshire, on the Wildcat River. I did a second one. You could do many, right from this spot. Of course I don't expect even an acceptable rough to be fully developed for color or atmosphere or climax, and I often do better in my finishes than my feel-out sketches have promised. Every stage is a creative stage.

69

[127]

[128]

The roughness that I started out with in my color mini continued on into the finish. Somehow an "unfinish" seemed to fit these old North Adams, Massachusetts, buildings better. What added a little extra enchantment to the view was the maple tree, with its remaining leaves ablaze with sunlight. I felt I ought to pick up this ultralight and let it carry across the sky breaking behind the buildings. Sometimes all I get time for are color roughs, with side notes for later finished paintings.

I did six scribble sketches this day from a moving motorboat on Long Island Sound, out toward Centerport. You take a couple of quick looks and you let that pencil fly. It's the best practice I know, something like doing one-minute sketches of the nude model. It was only later in this case that I made color roughs from my notes, and, from some of those, finished paintings. This way the painter just has to paint it broad, and that often results in a more suggestive painting.

70

[129]

[130]

This is the model's last pose of an evening of quick poses, and since it's usually a (long) twenty-minute pose, she prefers this reclining posture. It gives her a chance to sleep. While a twenty-minute pose is relatively a quickie, *it has to be painted for its own sake* rather than as preparation for a later finished painting. In my color painting, after I had the pencil guidelines done, I in one wetting got in most of the model, and one more wetting took care of the background. It has to be apparent, without comment, what I decided to play up.

Put the main interest where you want it. The journey up the road to the house was to be interesting but not enough to detract from the house as major interest. I slanted my two largest trees out, to open up the house area and cover over some of the road at bottom. As in my wash sketch and diagram with arrow. If I wanted to make the road more important than the house, I would do as in diagram marked "no," which reverses the slant of the two trees, thus blocking out the house.

71

[131]

[132]

Here are the glads we sketched a while back, and now you see how the contrast process works out in watercolor tones. To make one part stand out as our peak of interest—the left-hand glads—(1) we used our darkest background against the white—and less dark against the remaining white flowers. (2) In addition, we washed in a light gray tone on the right-hand flowers, reducing the contrast still further. Another emphasis (3), I delineated more sharply in the left-hand glads the pistils sticking up from the flower-petal pocket.

This action is a favorite that so many painters like to copy. Marine painter Stanley Woodward in his advice to painters recommended studying the sea. Get down there and look by the hour. Paint the sea and rocks and islands in all kinds of weather. *Don't copy someone else's work or use photographs.* Even if you make a "non-subject" of it, get the thrill of feeling that you're painting and creating so others can share your discoveries.

72

[133]

[134]

Bonus assignment ⚹1: Do a rough in black-and-white, making sure your tone areas contrast. Use a scribble sketch as your model, one of mine or your own. Then do a full-color version, seeing that your color tones are pretty much the tones you used in your black watercolor. Don't hesitate to change a tone to suit your purpose—like making a light roof dark, as I have. Now do another making your major touching areas too nearly alike in tone (top one). Knowing how to kill a picture—and actually doing it—helps you make one come alive.

Bonus assignment ⚹2: On a discarded piece of rough-textured paper, do a whole sheet of varieties of tone—some in black, some in light colors, some in dark colors: (a) the flat wash on a dry surface, leaving white flecks; (b) irregular washes you get from turning your brush and varying the pressure [Frame 100]. (c) Try putting another brushful of same tone paint into and over a painted section still wet. (d) Try stroking some darker paint over a painted section already dry.

73

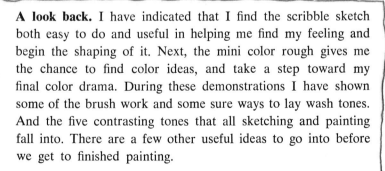

[135]

[136]

A look back. I have indicated that I find the scribble sketch both easy to do and useful in helping me find my feeling and begin the shaping of it. Next, the mini color rough gives me the chance to find color ideas, and take a step toward my final color drama. During these demonstrations I have shown some of the brush work and some sure ways to lay wash tones. And the five contrasting tones that all sketching and painting fall into. There are a few other useful ideas to go into before we get to finished painting.

A look ahead: "light" as part of every step of watercolor painting. Light, whether sunlight or artificial, affects (a) what you see, (b) how you see, (c) what you sketch and paint, (d) the colors you use, (e) your contrasts. Essential as it is, light is the simplest element of painting. It's easy to understand and utilize, once you are reminded of the kinds of lighting, what they do for you, and what you can do with them—which is about what this next short chapter demonstrates.

Sketch, Santa Monica Beach, Santa Monica, California.

74

Session 6 Light molds your picture

How does Light help you shape your feeling?

Ways for you to control Light

[137]

[138]

Without light there is, of course, no picture. What you see—all quantity, all color, all form, all contrasts—is affected by quality and direction of light. Light isn't something you *do* (in the sense that you *do* scribbling or *put* paint on paper). All you do with light is observe it and consider how you want to use it. I think of light as not controlling you or your picture. It's you who control your light—you have options.

Light option ⚹1—finding the five tones. As an artist I don't want to know the science aspects of light. Light to me is half-shutting my eyes and finding the five tones I use in paint and pen-and-ink. That helps me understand why so much is happening in this watercolor adaptation of a picture not my own. The middle and dark mass tones comprising most of the picture are turned on by the brilliant lighting behind the clouds and its reflection in the wet beach, creating conflict and drama.

76

[139]

[140]

Options: Proportions of light and dark. The most widely used light is (a) three-quarter lighting—three quarters light and one quarter shadow. (b) This shows the reverse: one quarter highlight, three quarters shadow. Usually too much darkness for general use, but when this one-quarter highlight is repeated on several objects in the picture, it can form an interesting pattern.

Front lighting. (1) It floods your subject in a monotony of uniformly bright light, with very little shadow to bring out form. All-bright-light is as uninteresting as all-middle-tones in a painting. (2) *High overhead lighting,* as at noon outdoors, creates deep shadows under the eyes, nose, and cheekbones—seldom an interesting effect. Noon lighting throws light high on trees, shadows the trunks, casts almost no shadow. Usually dull. Also doesn't do much for your sky. The artist deals largely in middle tones plus smaller areas of highlights and shadows.

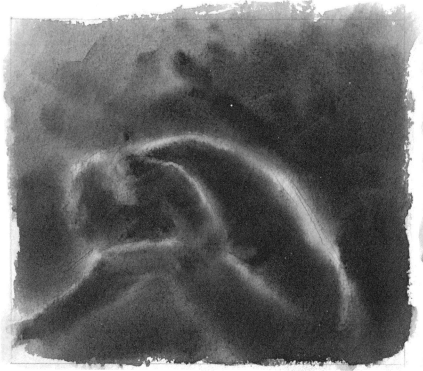

[141]

[142]

Side-lighting, rim-lighting, and back-lighting all have something in common: They throw a small border of light on the subject, and this can at times be very effective. I have thought for long about a feature watercolor back-lighting a nude model (meaning the principal light is behind the model). The foreground flesh tones in shadow would be a tone darker than the background, and the only bright lighting would be in the rim highlights.

Option: Controlling light position. *Indoors,* you usually can move it to suit. *Outdoors,* you can usually move yourself to a move favorable position. Or you do as I did in Central Park. I wanted the brilliant east light of summer's dawn coming from behind landmark buildings on Fifth Avenue, and reflecting in the lake inside the park. So I came back at dawn. *A moving light:* The sun as it moves changes your highlight, as on a tree. You anticipate the change, arranging your painting position accordingly. I always feel extra good when I'm all that smart.

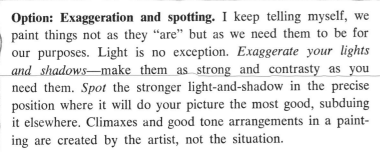

[143]

[144]

Option: Exaggeration and spotting. I keep telling myself, we paint things not as they "are" but as we need them to be for our purposes. Light is no exception. *Exaggerate your lights and shadows*—make them as strong and contrasty as you need them. *Spot* the stronger light-and-shadow in the precise position where it will do your picture the most good, subduing it elsewhere. Climaxes and good tone arrangements in a painting are created by the artist, not the situation.

Option: Racking up your lights and darks. You may do as you wish with lights, have them strike where you want them, from anywhere you want, and with the intensity you desire. It is pretty much up to you. But all your lighting should look as though it had the same control, came from the same source. For example, if it's late afternoon, let your lighting throughout the picture say late afternoon, not some noon and some late afternoon. Famed art teacher Frank Reilly called it "racking up your lights."

[145]

[146]

Reflected light. We think of light generally as "single source" lighting, though there can be several lesser sources, especially indoors. A single light with nothing to reflect its brightness would make a two-tone picture—absolute light and absolute dark, as above. However, outdoors nearly everything reflects light to some degree, and as in Frame 146, the cast shadows are translucent. Light colors usually reflect more, dark colors less.

Cast shadows, ⚹1. Direct light casts shadows that sometimes add to a picture's interest. Outdoors, the sunlight is usually located outside the realm of your picture—back of your subject or back of you. You look through your viewfinder and you do not see the sun within the picture or overhead. When it is that way, outside, as in the diagram, the shadows cast (by trees, for example) are parallel, not converging. No one will challenge you if you do your shadows that way.

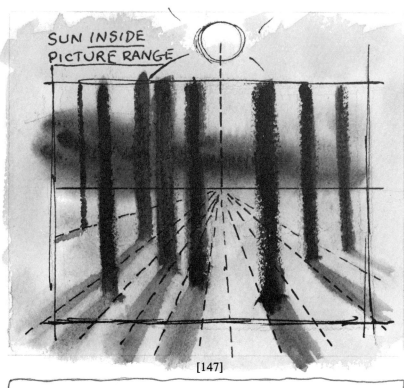

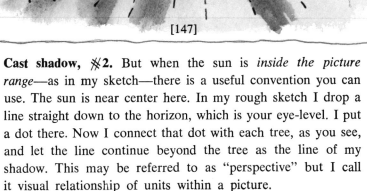

[147]

[148]

Cast shadow, ⅍2. But when the sun is *inside the picture range*—as in my sketch—there is a useful convention you can use. The sun is near center here. In my rough sketch I drop a line straight down to the horizon, which is your eye-level. I put a dot there. Now I connect that dot with each tree, as you see, and let the line continue beyond the tree as the line of my shadow. This may be referred to as "perspective" but I call it visual relationship of units within a picture.

Bonus assignment. Wherever you go, observe the effect of light around you. (1) Squint your eyes so everything is out of focus, see mass areas and the five 'tones of light and dark. (2) Occasionally use your sketchbook, do a scribble sketch or two, simply as tones of light, no detail. (3) Indoors or out, change your position in viewing an object, seeing it from front lighting to side lighting to three quarters, to one quarter. Observing light is one of your best preparations for painting.

[149]

[150]

A look back. There's a lot you'll experience about light as you get invoived with it in your painting. But nothing you need worry about or try to learn formally. Review the options once in a while and keep thinking about light and using it, and it'll grow on you. What we have arrived at is that light has to do with seeing, color, and the form of things, and that it's easy to use in your painting. And above all, you are the boss of light. You utilize it to serve you.

A look ahead. We've seen that mass areas are the structure on which you build your painting—from beginning to end. Nothing is more vital to painting. I find that people catch onto the mass way of painting and get good at it when they practice an exercise making "instant" pictures with abstract pieces of tone. It's a sort of game. You can do it with cutout pieces of paper or fabric. Or do it with quickie washes. In the next chapter, see which way works better for you.

Making pictures from 4 mass areas

Little switches change the picture *fast*

[151]

[152]

"Instant pictures." I originally devised the flannel-board demonstration so my live audiences of artists could see me put a picture together (size 36″ by 24″) with four or five different-tone pieces of felt in a few minutes—so they could judge quickly how the picture was coming along. Then, by switching a couple of the pieces, I could show them how a changed version looked. It was wonderful practice for me, and some of the people watching said they'd like to do it at home.

Now you can practice instant pictures too. I can't show here the dramatic action of manipulating pieces of fabric, but I can show you the action via quickie washes in a "step" series of pictures. Then you can either do it as I do—use washes—or, if you like, make a set of five tones on paper and cut them up into irregular shapes. Or use cut-up felt pieces, obtainable in many craft stores. *First stage:* A light gray for sky and water. A darker gray for shore. It's a picture all right, but apparently not much is happening.

[153]

[154]

A third tone is added: From the horizon down to bottom of picture, I have washed in a middle gray tone to indicate the body of water. The picture's interest has increased with this added tone. Even so, I have no center of interest, no one place for the viewer's eyes to catch on to. A finished painting in this spirit would end up nothing more than a junk inventory. *What was there about this sight that made me want to paint it?*

Now a high point of interest. The incoming tide was creating mild breakers all over the place, but they looked bigger where I stood. The setting plus the powerful Atlantic Ocean breaking against the resistant Maine coast rocks—that was it for me. I make sure the viewer's eyes go to the foreground of breakers and rocks by washing in (a) my lightest tone—(opaque) white, and (b) the largest area of it, though itself only a small area. But I want you to view the shoreline too, so I sprinkle smaller bits of white breakers.

85

[155]

[156]

Move the interest point. As the tide came in and the waves got stronger, I was attracted to nearer the middle of my picture, where I now indicate the big spray with an area of white. I have made all the other white tones throughout the picture smaller and scattered them out comet-fashion. The climax occupies a relatively small area, leaving plenty of the picture for the journeys of discovery that do so much to express your feeling.

Still another change in interest-climax. Following a storm, this brilliant sky broke through the medium gray storm clouds, silhouetting the far conifers. I transfer my white dominance to the sky, and I have put a small amount of darkest (black) on the skyline to complete the contrast. We make a fascinating trip into middle and foreground darker water, smaller breakers scattered comet-fashion, all these now secondary in interest yet still a vital part of my whole feeling.

86

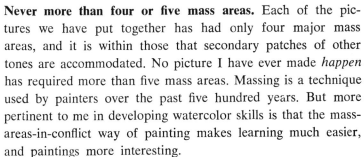

[157]

[158]

Never more than four or five mass areas. Each of the pictures we have put together has had only four major mass areas, and it is within those that secondary patches of other tones are accommodated. No picture I have ever made *happen* has required more than five mass areas. Massing is a technique used by painters over the past five hundred years. But more pertinent to me in developing watercolor skills is that the mass-areas-in-conflict way of painting makes learning much easier, and paintings more interesting.

Horrors can creep in. Lest I think making an organized picture is all that easy, I like to look at a horror example like this one where everything is turned on at once. Lightest areas scattered all over the place, mass areas filled in so they have lost their mass capacity to function. No discrimination, no selection, a patchquilt of junk. I call it a view without a viewpoint. Not only beginners make this mistake.

[159]

[160]

Another way to contrast your masses. In the demonstrations just finished, we adjusted mass tones to conditions that changed for us—weather, waves, sky. This time, without changing lighting or anything in the bouquet, see what we can do with our mass tones to help us toward a lively painting. The dark tones are [purple] iris, spikes, leaves. The light tones are [yellow] jonquils, the middle tone stands for background. Dull picture, don't you think? To get something going, what do I feel?

How about making jonquils the feature this time? I have placed a "darkest" tone right against the top-positioned two jonquils which I have made just a bit lighter. My dark tone meanders into the background at the left and on down near but not touching the other jonquils. That way my dark spotting doesn't look too contrived or "sudden." To keep the iris from challenging, I keep the contrasts around the iris at a minimum—dark gray against middle gray.

88

[161]

[162]

What do I do to make the iris take over? Retain the middle grays against the light gray of the jonquils, so they won't pop out. Create a mass of light, the lightest in the sketch, and put it behind the iris. Along with that, make parts of the dark-tone [purple] iris a little darker for more contrast. Let some of this dark splash into the other iris at the bottom. It doesn't there step up contrast or distract but does help form one of the several journeys of discovery that complete the picture.

Bonus assignment. (1) *In flat washes,* do one of my examples (or your own) step by step, placing the high point of interest one location then another. (2) Or do the same thing with cut-up pieces: Paint on 8 by 10 paper a set of the five [black] tones. Or use felt pieces in five tones. Scissor them up into a variety of shapes. Jockeying your masses (by wash or pieces) is good exercise to make you more conscious of masses and expert at the mass way of picture-making.

Session 8 *Pattern and texture for accent*

Finishing touches to make your picture *happen*

Ways to point up your pictures

Techniques

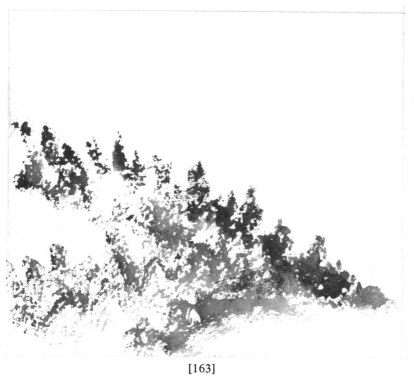

[163]

[164]

"Pattern" selected from mass areas. When you are skilled at "seeing," you see first the structure of your picture as a few major mass areas—no detail. Once you have your picture structured as masses, you focus on detail. You select what detail you need for the finishing touches. I classify such detail as *pattern*—the conifer trees in the Ocean Island picture, the shadows, the little touches that characterize and make a picture that much more interesting.

Two main uses of pattern. Here the selected bits of black pattern have been put in place over two different dark gray mass areas: (1) Against the bright sky, the black pattern collaborates for a strengthened contrast and high interest point of the picture. The one big thing the viewer sees first. (2) On the other hand, the same kind of black pattern farther down against the dark gray mass area forms little contrast. There it adds not contrast but character detail and interest.

[165]

[166]

Besides distant pine trees, what do I include as pattern? Branches of a tree, a fence, shapes of flowers, leaves close-up (as rhododendron leaves in a bouquet). Tree trunks against the water of the lake, the design on a jug and even the jug itself. The sailboat on the horizon, but in the harbor close-up the mast and the skipper. A distant fisherman but not one close-up. In the human figure, hair and facial features but usually not skin. *Pattern is largely accent.*

Texture, related to pattern, is usually a surface, and not in itself especially noticeable—as the irregularity of a meadow, skin or surface generally. Fabrics. Cloud variations, background behind a portrait and the frame itself. Pebbles on a beach, the grain on a rock and sometimes the rock. The barnside surface, the bark on a tree. The wrinkles in my pants and my face. All in all, any variations within mass areas would be either pattern or *texture.* To complete an area, characterize it, or point it up.

[167]

[168]

Freeform in pattern. Indicating your pattern roughly within your mass areas of your sketch helps you be freeform about it. It's good training for painting. I try to be just as freeform when I get the paintbrush in my hands. The tendency is to try to draw with the brush, to try to make trees look like a tree looks. You're dead in watercolor when you do that. Wriggle your trees in with your paintbrush, and they'll suggest trees to your viewers. Or if you use cut-out pieces for your massing, shred some bits and pieces to represent pattern.

Bonus assignment. On your practice mass areas, demonstrate to yourself the placement of small quantities of pattern to point up a contrast, and in other parts of the picture, use pattern to characterize or complete an area. Keep it rough Don't be tempted into doing a finish. Save finish—we're coming to it in the next session.

93

[169]

[170]

A look back. You've been exposed to nearly everything you need to know for making a finished watercolor painting: (a) Having a feeling for something and wanting to shape it in your painting for others to share. (b) A sure and easy way to get started: the scribble sketch. (c) Your color tryout and color itself. (d) Handling the brush and stroking. (e) You the boss over your light. (f) How much easier it is to deal in only four or five mass areas. (g) Using pattern to point up your picture and give it character.

A look ahead. To me, all of that adds up to 90 per cent of watercolor painting. As I get into my finished painting demonstrations, you may recognize the many things you have already done and learned or are familiar with. *Yet this last 10 per cent makes it or breaks it.* Get your blank sheet ready.

94

Session 9 The finished painting in Spotwet Watercolor

Theme and countertheme

Techniques for common situations

Successful painting sequences

Freshness the name of the game

Interesting watercolor effects

Tricks, devices, mistakes, antidotes

Subjects and non-subjects

[171]

[172]

Sebago Lake—color shot, Frame 122. This is a black-and-white mini color rough version of the on-the-spot painting I did for you back in the Color Session. I have selected this one for an extended finished watercolor demonstration because it puts to use a wide range of watercolor technique, and it puts to work many of the ideas we have so far gone into.

My feeling. I want to remind myself with this beginning of the scribble sketch that my feeling seemed to reach its peak with the foreground tree trunks in deep shadow, contrasted against the very (*lightest*) cool gray-blue of the lake. From there, my feeling included in a lesser way the sunny foreground with its tones of warm reds, oranges, yellows, browns, greens. And the tree foliage with its patches of sun coming through. To me it said lovely lakeside of a summer's day.

96

[173]

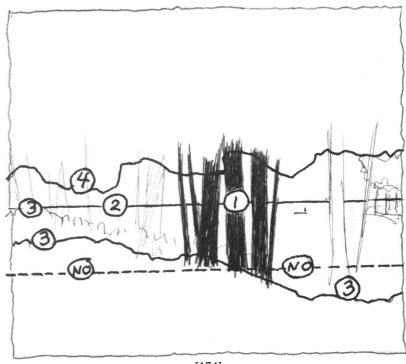

[174]

Pencil guide. Using my scribble sketch as a guide, yet looking out at the scene as well, I jot down in light pencil some indications of where things go—trees, foliage, shoreline, horizon. No drawing ability required, just observation. I want to be sure I'm doing not a detailed pencil drawing to be filled in with color but a watercolor painting. Sparse pencil guidelines force the artist to create visual interest out of paint-and-brush, mass areas, and painted pattern accents.

Several things I want to check about my pencil marks: (1) That tree trunks are longest and more concentrated toward the right. (2) That my lake-horizon line is below center so it doesn't cut my picture into equal halves. (3) That my foreground starts lower down in the picture on the right and goes higher up on the left. Why? Because one more "horizontal" line would give me two similar rectangular shapes out of my four. That would be dull. (4) I want to be sure most of my tree foliage lets the distant horizon be seen.

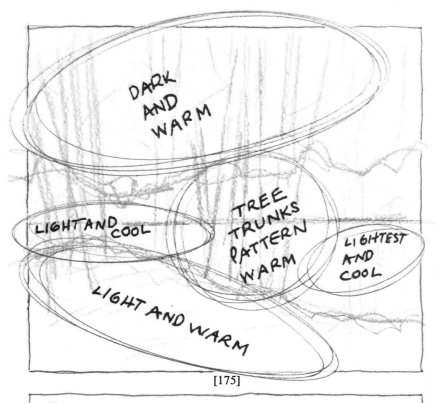

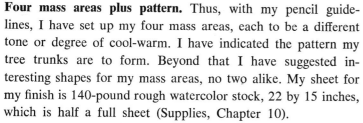

[175]

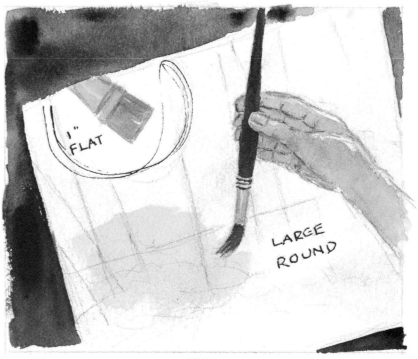

[176]

Four mass areas plus pattern. Thus, with my pencil guidelines, I have set up my four mass areas, each to be a different tone or degree of cool-warm. I have indicated the pattern my tree trunks are to form. Beyond that I have suggested interesting shapes for my mass areas, no two alike. My sheet for my finish is 140-pound rough watercolor stock, 22 by 15 inches, which is half a full sheet (Supplies, Chapter 10).

Spotwetting is wetting a section of the paper—in preparation for live, moist paint to be brushed in while the area is still wet. *Directions:* (1) With plain water, spotwet the desired area plus a few inches beyond all around. (2) Quickly do an even wetting, without puddles. (3) Use a large brush, flat or round.

98

[177]

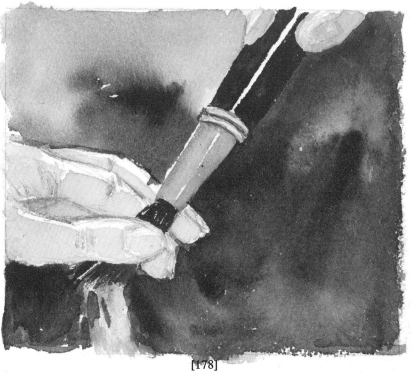

[178]

Paint into wet area . . . sensual. Your paper is level, the water is already on the paper, so this time less water is required on the brush. *Apply the paint promptly and keep painting while the surface remains wet.* The paint goes on "dryer" and does its mixing with water *on the paper*. It's a pretty simple idea. Yet this mingling on the wet paper leads to some of watercolor's most sensual appeal, and helps make it the fascinating medium it is.

Squeezing out your brush. You already know that the hair part of a good watercolor brush picks up more than its weight in water [Frame 93]. Dipping the brush onto the sponge to lose some of the water, ordinarily adequate, is not enough in this case. With your fingers, gently squeeze out much of the water. Gently, because those bristles are a delicate tool to you as much as a scalpel is to a surgeon. Then touch brush into the edge of your moist paint, picking up a "very little bit" of it. When you try it out you'll know how much a little bit is.

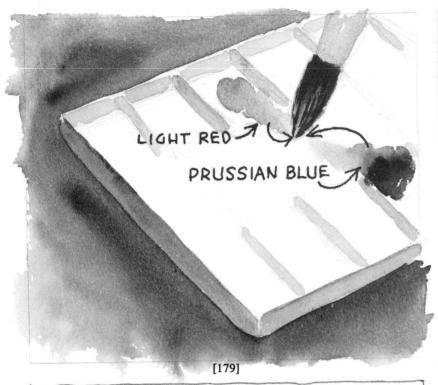

LIGHT RED

PRUSSIAN BLUE

[179]

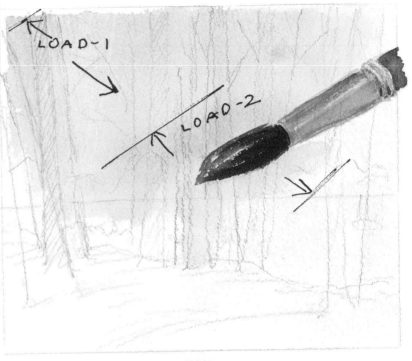

LOAD-1

LOAD-2

[180]

Blue-gray. The sky in our picture is very light, and although "blue," it's a grayed blue. Thus if I use a Prussian blue, I want to tone it down a very little—gray it—and a little light red does just that for you. When you're painting you do this subtle mixing in a twinkling and automatically. Test your paint pickup on the tryout sheet, where it will test out darker than it will be after it hits the water on the paper.

Washing into wet. *Load 1.* Starting at the top of your paper (sky), swish your brush back and forth without scrubbing around and without too much going back over. Make the wash-in even or uneven as you choose. *Loads 2, 3.* You'll need a few more brushfuls of (relatively dry) paint to complete the section. Get each load quickly, and work it promptly into where you left off, while it's *still wet.* If you wait too long to continue the tone and the area goes "almost dry," *wham!* You've created waterlogging, the greatest killer you'll run into.

KILLER:
"WATERLOGGING"

[181]

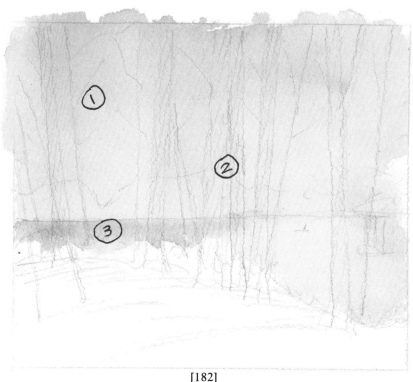

[182]

Waterlogging and stain-fencing. A killer of such magnitude is entitled to a rogue's-gallery shot all its own. How is it this picture killer is so devastating? Reason: The painted surface is almost dry—the paint is in a state of suspension, it has not completed its grip on the paper. A new flood of water streams in, pushing the almost-dry, suspended paint before it. The new water spreads and makes a washed-out basin, and all around it the displaced paint particles form kind of a stain-fence. [Frame 202 gives remedy.]

Timing and dryer paint. With a little practice, you'll find it easy to spotwet a section with plain water and promptly brush into it (1) from the top, the beginning of the sky, followed by (2) additional brushfuls to complete sky and lake. And then (3) at once while the brushed-in lake is still wet, a darker tone for the lake. Too large a spotwet area can dry out before you can get it painted. Or your sheet can curl. If it curls, keep on painting but start your drying period as soon as you can. Try it a few times.

101

[183]

[184]

Overpainting. Into the sky (upper left) you can put that cloud (second picture) in one of two ways: *Technique 1: While the sky is still wet,* with a fairly dry brushful of strong (dark in tone) paint—ultramarine blue and burnt sienna this time —firmly stroke the dark paint into your still-wet sky. Don't overwork it. Let the paint move around by itself, the way an actual cloud in the sky does.

It dries quite a bit lighter than it looks wet.

Overpainting, continued. *Technique 2.* Another way—and just as good—let your original sky dry fully. Be sure it is dry. Then gently and quickly with clear water and a one-inch flat brush spotwet the painted area, making sure you don't disturb the painted surface. *Wet a few inches beyond the cloud area.* Get a good charge of paint on your pretty dry brush and stroke it into the spotwet area. Don't overwork it. Practice it a time or two—it's not difficult. This is one of those rewarding effects so easy in watercolor and hard in any other medium.

102

SKY =
PRUSSIAN
BLUE
+TOUCH OF
LIGHT RED

TREES =
BURNT SIENNA
+ ULTRAMARINE
BLUE

THALO GREEN
+ YELLOW OCHRE

[185]

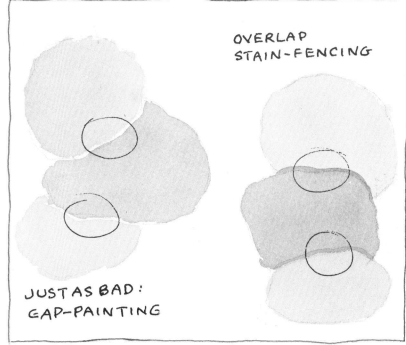

OVERLAP
STAIN-FENCING

JUST AS BAD:
GAP-PAINTING

[186]

Black + You = Color. In this kind of book most illustrations are in a single color (black) printing. In this case that's a break for the artist-reader seeking extra color experience. When I show the black tone and say in words the colors represented, I suggest you stop and recall to your mind what those colors look like. If you like, refer back to Session 4 on color, and see how close you are.

Gap-painting, stain-fencing. The other day I saw the watercolor attempt of a good oil painter. He laid each tone and let it dry—in each case tight up to the boundary line for the area. When he washed in the neighboring tone, he was very careful not to leave a white paper gap to separate his areas. Instead, he created undesirable stain-fencing from overlappings. He was insulting to the watercolor medium: He thought an oil painter could do watercolor without knowing its techniques, simple as they are. Stain-fencing removal: Frame 202.

103

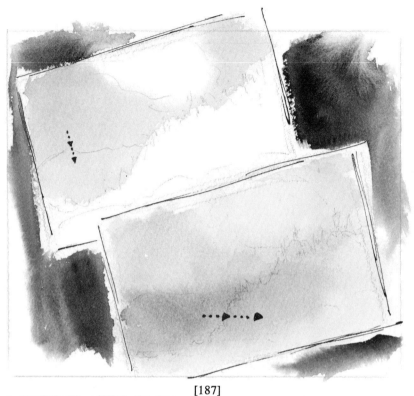

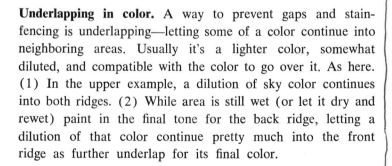

[187]

[188]

Underlapping in color. A way to prevent gaps and stain-fencing is underlapping—letting some of a color continue into neighboring areas. Usually it's a lighter color, somewhat diluted, and compatible with the color to go over it. As here. (1) In the upper example, a dilution of sky color continues into both ridges. (2) While area is still wet (or let it dry and rewet) paint in the final tone for the back ridge, letting a dilution of that color continue pretty much into the front ridge as further underlap for its final color.

Overpainting into wet. Over a still-wet sky-lake area, I have washed in a medium-tone gray-blue for the lake, darker toward horizon. (1) If my lake wash "leaks" a little into the sky area, that's a nice effect suggesting spontaneity and fresh-ness. If the horizon line needs strengthening, that's something to think about toward the end of the picture. (2) I let the bot-tom of it form its own irregular edge against the ground foliage, a good thing to do.

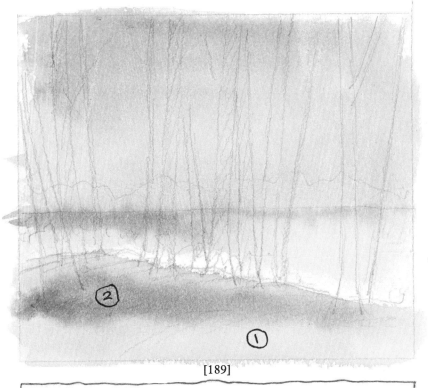

[189]

[190]

Washing one color into another. Since the foreground area does not touch lake area, I can do the foreground spotwetting without waiting for lake to dry. I follow the spotwetting at once with (1) a wash-in of yellow ochre. While that's still wet, with a squeezed-out brush wash in near the lake (2) a touch of light red and orange. It will dry lighter as all paint into wet areas does. Allow for it. Try this yourself a few times. Outdoors keep your paper as level as you can—so the wet paint won't wander around.

Drying time. I showed what happens to me when I let water-logging take over. Now with sky and lake and foreground washed in, I am ready to put in foliage, trees, bushes, branches, shadows—on top of what I have already painted. This calls for a halt to let the painted areas dry, to avert waterlogging. Set your painting aside, look over the scene, and give some thought to your next painting step. *About wrinkled paper:* Any time excessive water wrinkles your paper, *stop at once, let your paper dry, before resuming.*

105

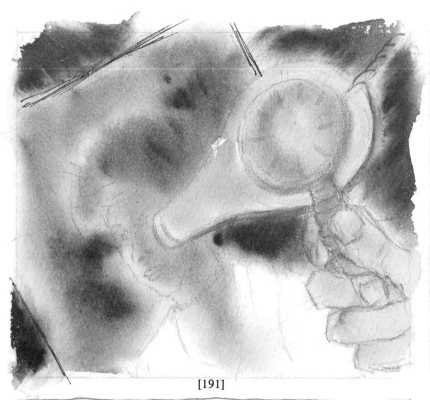

[191]

[192]

Dry-time as technique. A crucial part of watercolor painting is knowing when you need to take a time-out for drying, and being willing to. If you can and will utilize drying periods, you have learned one of the most useful techniques of the medium. Outdoors, five to ten minutes ordinarily dries my paper. Indoors I use a hair dryer to speed up the drying period. I can see by reflection which areas are still wet.

Spotwetting over painted area. After a plain-water spotwetting over the painted sky, I touch in good-size areas of yellow ochre as underpainting for the green foliage to go on top of it. For foliage I use a good charge of thalo green and burnt sienna on a fairly dry brush, turning my brush this way and that for un-even dark tones [Frame 100], some light, some darker, and the yellow ochre showing through as spots of sunlight. I have circled the areas where the underpainting of yellow ochre shows through.

106

[193]

[194]

Finishing the foliage area. For the extra darks—while the area is still wet—I brush in charges of dry paint, with very little water. Or let the area dry thoroughly, then rewet, and at once put in the darks. Try both ways, get good at this technique. Note that not a single leaf is painted in, yet the total suggests thousands of leaves to the viewer. This makes your painting something less than reality and at the same time something more.

Much in little time. Pausing to point out an advantage to watercolor. In just a few minutes I am able to wash in sky, lake, and a suggestion of leaves on the trees, all looking fresh and more like a concept of sky and lake and foliage than an hour or two of painting in a less flexible medium. Watercolor is a speedy medium, a suggestive medium that lets you come up with resourceful creativity. Speed and facility are especially desirable when you're painting outdoors with the light changing by the minute.

107

[195]

[196]

Variety of browns, in the tree trunks and some of the branches higher up, introduces another useful technique. With the sheet dry, I am using an ultramarine blue mixed with burnt sienna for most of the tree trunks, in varying combinations. Sometimes the blue predominates, sometimes the brown. For variety in other tree trunks I add a very little alizarin crimson. In my way of painting, it would be an artistic crime to mix up a whole batch of dark brown and make all the tree trunks alike.

Two-color "skip-stroking." With a medium-dry brush I have picked up ultramarine blue and burnt sienna on the same brush. (a) My brush is almost horizontal to make some tree-shape kind of skip-stroking. (b) With little water in the brush and the brush upright, a useful stroke I refer to as "almost dry brush," I do thin branches. Both techniques are ideal and suggestive on a dry rough-texture sheet, where the brush skims across, leaving porous strokings of paint.

108

[197]

[198]

Pattern in "skip-stroking." The branches and tree trunks are what I call pattern-texture. Painted pattern to complete the mass areas. Usually in small quantities. The skip-stroking technique is used for many things: (a) irregular surface on a beach, or (b) as in fall leaves on the ground. Brush in a dilution of light red, let it dry, then skip-brush over it with a darker color. This leaves uncovered some of the undercoat of the light red to appear as leaf highlights. Done quickly and without overworking.

Skip-stroking pattern for contrast. I have skip-brushed the remaining branches and tree trunks, making darker those trunks that are to contrast most against the lightest tone of the lake. For the shadows under the trees, I spotwetted its area, and with burnt sienna and a touch of ultramarine blue, I have washed in a small middle tone of shadow. Letting it dry, I have painted some shadows in a lighter tone into the foreground area. *After an area is dry, another tone to darken it may be washed over it as needed.*

[199]

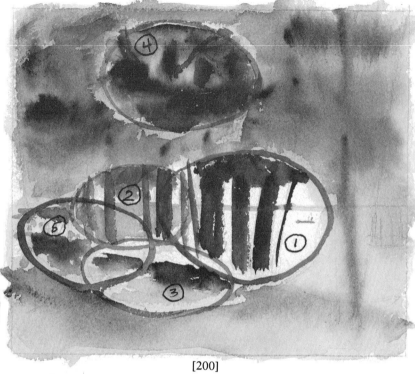

[200]

Brightest color pattern not dominating. Between foreground shadow and lake, I have painted on the dry surface a suggestion of bushes and grasses, using light greens, yellows, even a little red. In this picture, this is pattern. Although these are the brightest, undiluted colors in the picture, they add up to just an interesting touch of feeling and a journey of discovery. Why don't they dominate? Because they are not set up in severe contrast.

My feeling takes shape in my painting. I see (1) the area of darkest darks against the lightest light as the high point of my feeling, everything else being largely middle tones and interesting side trips: (2) The pattern of the remaining tree trunks left-center. (3) The pattern shadows under the trees in foreground. (4) The network of tree foliage, with the touches of sunlight and pattern branches. (5) The ground foliage—light greens, yellows. And the over-all warm color— all adding up and reflecting my feeling.

110

HARD (SHARP) EDGES

SOFT, FADE-OUT

[201]

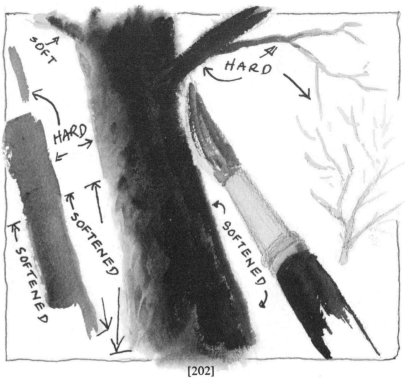

SOFT

HARD

SOFTENED

SOFTENED

HARD

SOFTENED

[202]

Sharp edges (hard) into fade edges (soft). I have made some of the tree trunks sharp-edged, so I can show how to soften what is often called a "hard" edge. *Hardly ever does anything appear to our eyes as sharp line or hard edge,* and in watercolor painting it's easy to let our masses and most patterns end in soft or fade-out edges. Branches are easier to put in sharp. To hold them back, I paint them grayed or off-color, like purple or blue, and often stroked into damp areas for further diffusion. Usually freeform.

To soften a hard edge. Clean your brush free of paint, and squeeze out much of the water. Draw the point of brush back and forth slowly over the hard edge and adjoining area. You'll learn how to draw it back and forth gently, until it picks up or loosens some of the edge paint, making the edge lighter in tone, and therefore softer. *Stain-removal:* Pick up unwanted stains or tones the same way, blotting up the wet and the loosened paint with a clean, dryer brush, blotter, towel, or Kleenex. Do until desired effect.

111

[203]

[204]

Decisions all the way. Nothing was automatic about this painting. I kept running into things to be decided—shapes, colors, patterns, contrasts high and low. I let some chrome yellow and more warm burnt sienna get into my tree foliage. I put some color variety into my tree trunks, and I let some trees come darker and the lake lightest in the high-interest area, where also I eliminated some of the competing shoreline foliage and the unnecessary activity in the rest of the foreground.

Further decisions: panning versus painting. Often I make a preliminary rough that seems all right, and I may even get through the finish, when I wonder what's the point of it. It turns out to be a junk-inventory picture, like this rough where the whole colorful scene seemed paintable. I overlooked that it wasn't even viewable as a single shot, that my eyes took in the panorama as a series of pictures. In painting, I prefer to forgo the heroic shot, the vast panorama.

112

[205]

[206]

How to check up on a flop painting. I have saved many a painting by: (1) Viewing it from fifteen feet, with half-shut eyes—do I have not over four mass areas? Do I have a high point of interest? (2) Another way. I move around some loose strips of matting, hoping to find a picture within the picture—as here. Often I recover the thing that fascinated me in the first place but that I had let slip away. From that fresh start I do another finished painting. Confidentially, some of my best paintings come that way.

Creativity turned on. In painting the new version, I knew my feeling hovered around the shining red-orange leaves area. My fingers and my Creativity Compartment took over and provided me with dark green-and-burnt sienna mass to bring out my light red leaves. That plus the upright tree trunk gave me my high point of interest. My Creativity Compartment further dictated the middle-gray fence to be against a field of light warm green. That was a real find. All now shaping my feeling for Sagamore Hill that bright fall day.

113

[208]

[209]

Ultrawet way. As I began a painting of Spectacle Islands at Boothbay Harbor, Maine, the six children watching me were banned by the father—so they wouldn't "bother the artist." Nevertheless, they watched my every stroke from the house, via binoculars. They wouldn't leave until they found out how I'd make a painting from those few pencil guidelines and paper so soaked in water it splashed. (Ultrawet Action Painting method has a single thorough soaking that has to last through the entire painting.)

Watercolor methods. I mention the beautiful Ultrawet (which I use much of the time) because out of it has come this Spotwetting technique. Spotwetting yields virtually every effect inherent in Ultrawet but is much easier to learn and use. Two other methods in general use are (1) relatively "dry" watercolor with little to no pre-wetting, and leaning toward hard edges and skip-brushing. (2) "Wet-in-wet," often with a wet blotter under a damp and angled painting sheet, an inadequate substitute for Ultrawet Action Painting.

Frame 207: Opposite, black-and-white version of full-color painting of Theodore Roosevelt's Sagamore Hill, Oyster Bay, Long Island.

[211]

[212]

Making your own background. Some student-painters panic when there is no drape background behind the jug of flowers. Create your own background to make your flowers do what you want. Decide where you need the darks and lights leading to your high moment and journeys of discovery, just as you do outdoors. Choose your colors to coincide with those background lights and darks. Painting flowers, gratifying in itself, is good indoor practice for outdoor painting—foliage, color, textures, pattern, growing things . . .

Non-subjects: skip the fussies. Not every subject is ideal for watercolor. This fujimum is a good example, as I see it. (a) I did those fussy petals in freeform stroking—in acrylic (oil all right too)—as opaque overpainting. In watercolor, as in (b) you'd have to leave the white spaces, and your painting could become contrived and tight. *I don't paint anything in watercolor that requires meticulous detail or careful outlining.* If the subject can't be freeform, to me it's not a subject for the kind of watercolor I'm talking about.

Frame 210: Opposite, Spectacled Islands, Boothbay Harbor, Maine.

[214]

[215]

Bonus assignment. On a sheet of rough watercolor stock: (1) Wet an area, and with squeeze-brush pick up a color or two, (a) brush into the wet. (b) Get a darker brushful and brush it in (keep it abstract). (2) Deliberately waterlog the area—overload your brush with water, and wash it into the almost dry area, creating stain-fencing. Let it dry, now repair it. (3) Do some skip-brushing. (4) Do some darker overpainting (fresh paint onto a painted area rewetted).

Bonus assignment de luxe: "non-painting" painting, a form of creativity. A jug of flowers or a something indoors or out that interests you. Relax, reflect, listen to the sounds, look a lot, feel it, smell it. Take it in. (1) Think of the first marks you'd make in your scribble sketch. (2) Half shut your eyes and mentally mass some of the areas. (3) What parts will be pattern? (4) Where could the interest peak come? (5) What colors would help bring out your feelings? *Do a non-painting once a week if you can.*

Frame 213: Opposite, black-and-white version of mums and snapdragons.

Creative guide to brushes, paint, and paper

Some other things you'll find useful

Things to make outdoor painting easier

GOOD BRUSHES AND A GOOD BRAND A "MUST"

Your dealer. I have usually relied on my professional art-supplies dealer for guidance in brand, kind, and quality of brushes. He knows his merchandise and the artist's requirements, and he is aware he makes more repeat customers by being a reliable consultant. He's helped me a lot.

Kinds of brushes. For fineline work, pure sables of a good brand are to me worth their price. However, for my kind of non-fussified watercolor painting, the brush experts and dealers have recommended to me "sabeline" (often either oxhair or a combination of sable-oxhair) as being flexible and responsive, yet resistant, durable, and more moderate in cost.

Sizes. I recommend as one of your creative acts the selection of larger sizes. Using the larger sizes, you are more likely to get your paint onto the paper more readily and with more freshness and spontaneity. I have never seen anyone do exciting watercolor with a small brush. On the other hand, I see show-offs (in demonstrations) mess up their paintings with brushes big enough to paint a small house.

This is what I go with: *Round:* #10, 14, 18. And for an occasional fineline touch, a #5 or 6. *Straight-flats:* 1½ inch, 1 inch, ½ inch. See if any of that suits you.

KEEP YOUR BRUSHES FIT TO USE

Clean after each using. Clean in mild soap and cool (never hot) water. Stroke brush gently into soap, get lather, then under water tap, flush it out in the palm of your hand. Repeat the process until water leaves your brush clear, free of soap and paint color. With fingers, gently squeeze out most of the water, shape brush back to normal. Paint, if left inside the hair area, cakes up and bulges hair out of place, making painting precarious. I use my watercolor brushes only for watercolor, never for acrylics or oil.

Storing. Let clean brush rest on handle, not on hair part. Let it dry before storing.

Long Life. Care gives me my money's worth out of my brushes. And yet, eventually, they do wear out, to the point where they affect my painting. Out they go. I replace at once—I like to continue to have enough brushes around me.

WATERCOLOR STOCK—KIND, SIZE, WEIGHT

To hold water. Watercolor stock is specially constructed to accept a coat of plain water and hold it while paint is applied. And then dry back to its original condition. Other kinds

Frame 216: Opposite, looking out our dining room window.

of paper—non-watercolor papers, however good they may be—can handicap you and nullify your best efforts. Your art-supplies dealer can help in the selection of suitable water-color stock.

Rough surface. For the kind of watercolor we're talking about—a combination of wet and dry stroking—only "rough" surface will do. Very rough or moderately rough—take your choice. I prefer moderately rough. But never the one called *smooth*. That is a different breed of watercolor that I seldom get into.

Size. Rough watercolor stock comes in sheets—40 by 27 inches, and the commoner size approximately 22 by 30. Finished paintings are done full-size but more frequently half sheet or 22 by 15, though the quarter sheet, 11 by 15, is also used for finishes. I recommend working no smaller than 22 by 15 for finishes. My sketches and mini color roughs are usually 11 by 15 or smaller.

Pads or blocks. Usually they are lightweight stock and bound on all four sides. It's convenient to carry, but unless you loosen three of the four sides as you use it, it wrinkles excessively when water hits it—largely because the bound sheet cannot expand properly.

Weight. Watercolor stock comes in a variety of weights (thicknesses). Try several, and see which you prefer. 140-pound (22 by 30) is generally a good weight for spotwet watercolor. 90-pound or 72-pound are almost as easy to use, especially after a painter is in control of the water. I haven't needed the costlier 200-, 300-, or 400-pound (very thick), though some of the top artists prefer it.

Paper-stretching, wetting and taping-down a lightweight stock, intended to prevent wrinkling, doesn't. I have never had to stretch paper (a great nuisance), nor do I know of any circumstance where I would need to.

Buy decent stock or forget watercolor painting. What is called an all-rag watercolor stock—the best made—can under ordinary circumstances last more than a hundred years without falling apart or losing its whiteness the way sleazy sheets do. Also a good sheet has a good surface-calendering and tooth that accept the paint and keep it "on top" for maximal brilliance. Good paper costs so little per painting anyway, I can't afford to have a cheap sheet kill me.

I buy sheets in full size and by the quire. Generally painters buy a half dozen or fewer sheets at a time. They cut it into halves or quarters as needed.

PAINT. WHY SELECT A GOOD BRAND?

The good watercolor paints have an efficient binder to hold them to the paper, and they are likely to retain their color and brilliancy, be good mixers, and continue dependable and consistent. Your art-supplies dealer usually is your best counsel in brand selection. But don't expect a color in one brand to be the same as another brand's. There is no uniformity among brands—each manufacturer has his own idea of what light red or burnt sienna or all-purpose basic green should look like. To get the same thing each time, stay with the one brand that satisfies you.

Watercolor paint goes far and costs so little. Using the best brands, I use up only three or four cents' worth of paint per painting. It doesn't pay me to take a chance on "bargain" paints. I use the regular tubes, which are about three inches long and narrow, and sometimes the two-inch fatter, more expensive "professional" tubes when I want special colors.

Paints in tubes, not in cakes. Fresh from the tube, paint is moist, soft, and full-bodied, and to me a necessity for spotwet watercolor. Each time I paint I squeeze out just a little fresh paint of the colors I am going to use. Not too much—it dries up on the palette.

And with a few drops of water I moisten paint that is still on my palette from last time. Every once in a while I scrape off all the paint residue. Too long on the palette, it dries into flakiness and loses its binder.

I prefer small tubes, replacing them as needed, since even in tubes the paint dries out. Still, I want never to be out of a color, especially if I am on a trip. So I carry spares of the colors I use most. I check my supplies a day before.

In preference to buying a "set" of paints, I recommend buying the desired colors. I like the combination I am listing. Try these or get your dealer's recommendation or work out a combination of your own. Your palette becomes your own personal thing.

It is to be noted that some colors are called dyes, which to me means they run faster when they hit water, and when mixed with other paints they sometimes separate. The dye paints are not as "thick" as some others, and not as opaque. Alizarin crimson is one of those, as also are thalo green, and Prussian blue (but not so much ultramarine blue); and black seems to separate and run some.

Polymer acrylic paints may be used for spotwet watercolor. There are advantages and disadvantages—like you have to be sure you keep your brushes wet while in use, and wash them out, or the acrylic turns them into permanent cement-like nonbrushes. As color, acrylic is said to be more brilliant, and when dry certainly it is more "durable" and water-resistant. For example, one wash may be laid on top of a dry tone without the under one dissolving or running. However, I have found that a tone does not always lay smooth, it may bubble. Acrylics are something new in the paint world and they're worth finding out about. Try a tube or two, read the literature available at your art dealer's, and see how acrylic works for you.

REDS

Alizarin crimson, essential, indispensable to my palette.
Deep red. You can mix it on your palette—alizarin crimson and medium red. I carry it already mixed.

Medium red. My basic red.

Light red. I carry it, I use it frequently. It can, however, be mixed on your palette: medium red with a touch of medium yellow (not lemon yellow, which is greenish).

Orange. I carry it though I don't use it very often. I can make it with medium red plus more medium yellow than is used for making light red. Sometimes right on the palette I add a little orange to my light red, or, using orange, I add a little light red to it. A painter seldom uses a paint without tempering it with something else or diluting it.

YELLOWS

Medium yellow. This is my basic yellow.

Light yellow. A little extra water in medium yellow would come pretty close to making it "light." However, I like to have light yellow as it comes, especially when I paint outdoors or do flowers. For some flowers a *lemon yellow* is needed (or some of the other specials like rose madder or magenta).

Yellow ochre. This is a good neutralizer—I slip it into many different colors as a "slow-down."

BASIC GREEN

Thalo green. One manufacturer calls his basic green thalo, another calls something like it hooker's green. I use either one as the basis for anything green but almost never "as is"—

123

Bernard Klonis used to say it was too "acidy." I get countless different "greens" by mixing with it almost any other color—yellow ochre, raw umber, burnt sienna, alizarin crimson, light red, medium yellow, black, Prussian blue or ultramarine, even orange. This way you get hundreds of greens.

THE BLUES

Prussian blue. This blue tends toward greenish, as you see dramatically when you mix it with burnt sienna for a gray or colder brown or warmer blue: It gives a greenish tinge. But Prussian blue is marvelous for skies, and with light red a beautiful slightly gray blue that many viewers respond to.

Ultramarine blue, on the other hand, is a purplish blue in most watercolor paint lines. It mixes with not too much effect with medium yellow for a green, but to perfection with burnt sienna for those grays and deeper browns I like so much. To make a purple or lavender, ultramarine and alizarin crimson are mates. It is to be noted that I do not carry a purple as such. It would dry out in my box before I'd get around to using it straight—and anyway, it would never be the required shade.

There is a cobalt blue, and of course other blues like cerulean (which is usually ultramarine blue plus white paint).

THE BROWNS

You could carry many (and I suggest that at least once you try some others). I use *burnt sienna* often and find it indispensable. I could make it each time but what a nuisance.

Raw umber, which varies so much by brand, is something like yellow ochre (browner though) in its function. I carry it, but unless you find a special use for it here and there as I have, you don't really need it. The same with *burnt umber* only more so. How often do you need a ready-mixed dark brown when you make it so easily with burnt sienna plus ultramarine or black.

Black. Some watercolor instructors disdain black, but I haven't found a good reason for not using it. Black does a lot to change many a color in a jiffy—whereas getting the same evolved color by other means takes more playing around than I have time for when I'm in glide.

Any other colors you like or need. If you develop a lot of use for any of the dozens of other less basic colors—naples yellow, Indian red, mauve, Paine's gray—stock the tube. I remember the day when the art-supply store at Art Students League had a run on naples yellow. What caused it? In Mr. Klonis' noon demonstration he mentioned naples yellow as part of a flesh tone he was laying. Wham!

White. It's not in my palette—though it's in my box of "spares." White as white or as a mixer is not acceptable in the kind of watercolor painting we've been working on. Your paper is white, and utilizing the white of paper for your white function gives you a more shimmering painting. White, being opaque, destroys that transparency. That's my main reason for not using white. But for repairs, that's something else. For example, in a finished painting I'm pleased with, I see one little thing I'd like to repair. I could wipe it out and risk a damage I may not ever be able to rectify. Or I could make a little opaque paint—white and something—that I can put over the little thing that annoys me. Bing, I do it. And nobody ever knows. Some painters may squirm over such sacrilege . . .

OTHER SUPPLIES AND MATERIALS

A paint box. Your art-supplies dealer carries many kinds. I like one just about large enough to hold my tubes of paint, three or four brushes, some pencils, a tiny pencil sharpener, a soap eraser and a more abrasive one, scribble pen or nylon-nibbed pen, a small palette that is part of the box. A box I can work from at home or away.

I keep a small hand towel stuck in my belt whenever I

124

paint. For cleaning or drying my hands and sometimes the brush. I may even mop up my table with it. I send towels to the laundry . . . they must wonder.

A 10 by 14 white semi-opaque layout pad (20-pound paper, good tooth-surface for pencil or pen—not ultrasmooth).

Pencils: soft 1-b, 2-b, and hard 1-h. Pen and holder: Speedball round-tip pens B-4, 5, 6. And regular round-pointed (not sharp) pens medium, such as the Hunt Artist Pens. I seldom need a very fine pen. Black India ink. Sketching nylon-nibbed pen—I keep buying all kinds. Some such pens are labeled "watercolor" meaning the ink in them; others are waterproof; and I don't know whether any are guaranteed to make an impression that won't soon fade with time. I do my "immortal" work not with that kind of ink but with India ink which is supposed to last. That's a consideration when you're selling an ink sketch. I sketch a lot with a ball-point pen (I have one medium, one fine) with refillable cartridges of waterproof India ink (Taubman brand). Not available everywhere.

A 9 by 12 sketchbook for freeform sketching. I keep several on hand, some pocket size, some larger. All with good surface for pen and pencil but not necessarily for watercolor. The paper should be perhaps twice as thick (heavy) and stiff as a sheet of typewriter paper.

Two small plastic water containers—one for pre-wet, one for painting and cleaning the brush. (When water-in-use gets too dirty for you, maybe once a painting, change it.) 3 by 5 cellulose sponge. For indoor use, an electric hair dryer. Not mandatory but a nice tool for fast drying indoors, especially on damp days. But also it "freezes" some of the effects as you desire them.

FOR OUTDOORS

I don't know how else I'd carry my outdoor materials if I didn't use a vinyl (attaché) case with handle, 19 by 14 by 3¾ or similar. It holds pads, sketchbook, pens, towels, paint box with paint, palette, and brushes, etc. It holds 16½ by 12½ tempered masonite boards or ordinary cardboard—one to put my paper on (over an opened-up stool) when I paint, one to put my paints, brushes, and water on beside me. It holds cut-up watercolor stock, size 15 by 11, along with my plastic water container, its top, a cellulose sponge. My viewer. Lap cloth. A small piece of soap wrapped in foil. This case and a canteen of water would be all you'd need if you traveled on foot, no car.

Further for outdoors (assuming you use car). A two-quart canteen with carrying strap (I carry two such canteens filled with water for a full day's painting). Or use a discarded plastic jug such as for bleach. I carry three lightweight portable folding chairs, one with a back, two without. A thermos of beverage, and almost always a sandwich. If I am traveling by car, I can carry also larger paper stock—22 by 15 and a backing large enough to support it, such as tempered masonite or a ferrotype (photographer's) tin.

For a take-off on foot. I load everything into a two-wheel folding wire shopping cart, and push it ahead of me as I walk and look in comfort. I carry in the car a portable lightweight table I designed. It's big enough to take even a full 30 by 22 sheet, and there's a pull-out ledge to hold paint palette, water container, sponge, brushes, pencil. The table has adjustable screw-on legs, so that I can make my table-top level on uneven ground surfaces. I need the table-top level when I do Ultrawet Action technique or my painting would flow away. Ultrawet Action painting calls for one more item: a small carpenter's level.

125

Be your own critic—judge your finished pictures

Ways to correct mistakes

Know when you've got a picture that *happens*

Purposes of this check-list guide. To help you (1) Judge your finished picture as your teacher might—that it checks out just fine or that it could be improved. (2) Locate error (if any). (3) Quickly locate specific help if you need it—to direct you to a single frame for a remedy or to a collated combination of frames.

How to use guide. (1) Whether your painting appears good to you or you are not sure about it, make it a habit to check it against the main group of check guides. (2) Read this section through occasionally, to be aware of its overall content and usefulness to you—(a) its main group of checkpoints, such as brush and painting techniques, color, feeling, picture-killers, massing, peak of interest (climax), etc.; and (b) its individual-item listings such as waterlogging, softening hard edges, re-wetting a painted surface, etc. (3) Turn to the designated frame or related series of frames, and replay the demonstrations. (4) If "doing something" is indicated—like putting a darker tone into an already wet lighter tone—practice it before applying it to your painting. (5) If a whole new painting seems the simplest solution, think of the new painting not as doing something over or a nuisance, but as learning into yourself another painting skill—all part of the joy and satisfaction of finding your feeling and shaping it for viewers to share.

MAIN CHECKPOINTS

Climax or peak of interest. Is there one most dominant area—the thing you see first from fifteen feet away? Does it symbolize your feeling, climax it?

Journey of discovery. Once you have the climax area, does your painting make clear the secondary points of interest, for the viewers' eyes to rove to? Does some background or secondary area seem too dominant?

Tone contrasts. Are the major tones not over four or five? Are they different in tone? Do two major tones meet in conflict and are they sufficiently different for maximal contrast? Do the middle tones prevail as they should over most of the picture's total area?

Masses. Can you half shut your eyes and pick out mass areas—not over four, at most five? Is picture broken up into too many smaller areas? Does the picture delineate too much?

Patterns. Have you utilized patterns within the climax area to build up major contrast? Elsewhere have you used your pattern for interest and not dominance as you should?

Lighting. Are your main highlights strong enough, are shadows dark enough, for contrast? Did you let your light come from a direction best for your picture and your feeling? Are your lights consistent—do they rack up?

Color. Have you stayed pretty much with one main color scheme or have you used too many this time? Have you made color help you express your feeling? Have you used your color in terms of grayness versus non-grayness—one good way for color interest and effectiveness.

Brush and painting techniques. Do any sections look overworked—like too much going back over? Any waterlogging? Stain-fencing, gap-fencing, stains? Hard edges where they would look better soft?

"Drawing" with the brush. Too much meticulous delineation? Is pencil guide too prominent—looking like a color fill-in? Freshness—does it look like too careful stroking, not the appearance of sketchiness, suggestivity? Could some of the effects be accomplished with more economy of stroking—such as skip-brushing? Or with more "freeform" stroking?

Frame number indicated after listing unless page is specified.